the hypnoth

The Hypnotherapy Handbook

Edited by Ann Jaloba HPD, MNCH,

Fiona Nicolson HPD, MNCH

All rights reserved. No part of this publication may be reproduced in any form (including electronically) without the written permission of the copyright owner except in accordance with the provisions of the Copyright Designs and Patents Act 1988. Application for permission to reproduce should be directed to the publisher.
ISBN 10 1495436624
ISBN 13 9781495436628

Published by Helping Handbooks Publishing, 26 Tapton Mount Close, Sheffield S10 5DJ

copyright © Ann Jaloba Fiona Nicolson 2014
the moral right of the authors have been asserted

the hypnotherapy handbook

DEDICATION

We would like to dedicate this book to all our fellow hypnotherapists who are working to help people and bring professional hypnotherapy to the wider public. We hope the book makes a contribution to that journey.

CONTENTS

Foreword	11
Taking care of yourself	21
Marketing your new business	37
Treating anxiety	61
Smoking cessation	97
Weight loss and management	119
Dealing with phobias	137
An overview of pain	155
Irritable Bowel Syndrome	171
Useful websites	203

Contributors to The Hypnotherapy Handbook

All our contributors are expert in their fields. If you want to practise in these areas they can guide you in how best to help your clients.

Marketing your new business

Nicola Griffiths and **Deborah Pearce** are hypnotherapists who can jointly boast over 50 years of marketing experience. As well as running hypnotherapy practices, they also head up Therapists Marketing Solutions (TMS) which offers marketing courses for hypnotherapy students and practitioners. When Nicola and Deborah realised that over 90% of therapists fail in their first year of practice, they set up TMS to help practitioners and students learn how to attract more clients.

Amongst other roles, Nicola Griffiths was Online Marketing Manager for a FTSE 250 company, in charge of their website and online marketing initiatives.

She is qualified as a hypnotherapist and psychotherapist and is also Trustee for the Association for Solution Focused Hypnotherapy. Before qualifying in hypnotherapy and psychotherapy, Deborah Pearce worked as a senior manager for major national charities, responsible for a range of functions including PR and Marketing.

More information about Nicola and Deborah and TMS can be found at www.doyouwantmoreclients.com; Twitter @TherapistsMS; www.facebook.com/thetms.solution

Looking after yourself

Ann Jaloba has more than 30 years experience of writing, editing and authoring health and wellbeing journals, books and magazines. She has edited award winning journals for the Royal College of Nursing, including the best selling weekly *Nursing Standard*.

She currently edits *The Hypnotherapy Journal,* the leading journal in its field in the UK and the flagship publication of the National Council for Hypnotherapy.

She has recently written *FIRSTDays: how to set up a therapy business and stay sane*, to help new therapists through that tricky first year in business and is co-editor of this book. She is an accredited supervisor for the National Council for Hypnotherapy and runs SupervisionPlus, a service offering supervision, peer support, information and training to both new and established therapists.

Ann also owns a busy practice in south west Sheffield where she specialises in helping people deal with weight problems, anxiety and work-related stress.

More information about Ann can be found at www.wellthought.co.uk or at supervisionplus.org

Treating Anxiety

Fiona Nicolson runs hypnotherapy clinics in Henley on Thames and Harley Street, London and has a particular interest in working with anxiety and trauma.

As well as seeing private clients, Fiona works as a therapist for Anxiety UK, the largest organisation in the UK specialising in anxiety disorders.

Fiona also runs clinics for Jamie Oliver's Fifteen Apprentice Programme, working with the apprentices to help them reach their full potential. Fiona is a member of the Editorial Advisory Board for the National Council for Hypnotherapy and co-editor of this book

More information about Fiona can be found at www.fionanicolson.com

Smoking cessation

Cathy Simmons is the creator of The Simmons Method, a science-based approach to addiction. As well as working with individual clients at her London clinic, Cathy runs 'Get Complete Confidence working with Smokers' training in The Simmons Method for qualified hypnotherapists.

Cathy is a qualified hypnotherapy supervisor and was initially Director of Supervision and subsequently Director of Ethics for the National Council of Hypnotherapy. Cathy is also the specialist advisor on addiction for the National Council for Hypnotherapy.

More information about Cathy can be found at www.cathysimmons.co.uk and you can follow Cathy on twitter on @cathy_simmons

Weight loss and management

Steve Miller is the UK's renowned weight loss coach, hypnotherapist and media personality. In 2010 Steve became the presenter of the hit TV show Fat Families on Sky Living, he is featured widely by the press and was recently branded the Simon Cowell of the Slimming World. In 2014 Steve was appointed celebrity blogger to The Huffington Post and the weight loss expert for Hello Magazine online.

Steve is a published author and is director of the Hypnotherapy Business School which offers business and marketing education

for hypnotherapists and is a specialist advisor to the National Council for Hypnotherapy.
More information about Steve can be found at www.yourweightlossmaster.com; www.hypnotherapybusinessschool.co.uk; Twitter @steve___miller

An overview of pain

Clem Turner is an experienced clinical and cognitive behavioural hypnotherapist and is an accredited member of the National Council for Hypnotherapy and a senior member of the General Hypnotherapy Register. Clem runs practices in Sutton in Ashfield as well as Mansfield in Nottinghamshire, specialising in Pain Management, Stress and Anxiety Management and also Irritable Bowel Syndrome.

Clem is a certified provider of The Listening Programme (a programme to help children with learning difficulties) with Advanced Brain Technologies.

Together with his wife Margaret, who is also a qualified and practising hypnotherapist, Clem runs a range of continuous professional development workshops which are recognised by the General Hypnotherapy Register and National Council for Hypnotherapy.
More information about Clem can be found at www.clemturner.co.uk www.clemturner.co.uk/trainingworkshops.htm

Irritable Bowel Syndrome

Since qualifying as a hypnotherapist and stress management coach, **Debbie Waller** has run a busy hypnotherapy and stress management practice in Yorkshire, UK. Although she sees people with other issues, she has a particular interest in working with stress and the related areas such as phobias, anxiety and Irritable Bowel Syndrome. She works mostly with one to one clients but also regularly provides seminars and stress management training to local businesses and groups.

Debbie taught for a nationwide therapy training organisation for three years alongside her therapy practice before launching her own school, Yorkshire Hypnotherapy Training. She currently divides her time between working with clients, training therapists and running an online magazine for student and practising hypnotherapists.

More information about Debbie can be found at
www.debbiewaller.com
www.hypnotherapy-for-ibs.co.uk
www.yorkshirehypnotherapytraining.co.uk
www.facebook.com/DebbieWallerHypnotherapy

Phobias

Pat Duckworth is a Cognitive Hypnotherapist, award winning author and public speaker.

Pat sees clients on a one-to-one basis at her therapy rooms in Harley Street, London, Cambridgeshire and Toronto. She has delivered training and workshops on a wide range of well-being subjects.

Pat has worked successfully with clients experiencing a diverse range of phobias from the more common spiders and dogs through to black barns.

More information about Pat can be found at
www.patduckworth.com

Foreword

by Dr Brian Roet

The Hypnotherapy Handbook is more than it states. A handbook is a book giving brief information, such as the basic parts of a subject. The Hypnotherapy Handbook is much more.

I believe it is actually a Manual—a book giving instructions and information—a 'How To' book, and is much the better for this.

The word "hypnotherapy" can be very confusing for clients seeking help. Many believe they will bring their symptoms to the therapist, sit down, close their eyes, and when they open them will be cured by "hypnotherapy"!

Hypnotherapy is a therapy using hypnosis alongside many other aspects of counselling and psychotherapy. This book includes the many parts of therapy that blend with hypnosis, and so is an ideal book for those who wish to practise using all the components involved in "hypnotherapy".

I have been practising hypnotherapy for more than 40 years, yet I found this book provided many insights that I was unaware of; different ways to assess a problem and tailor a treatment for it.

I use the word "tailor" intentionally, as I believe treatment should be "tailored" to the client, just as a suit should be tailored for the customer. In order to tailor the treatment (or suit) we need to know about the client (customer).

Learning many ways to help your client, means you are in a

better position to be of value to whoever seeks your help. This book provides the reader with alternative ways to view the problem and construct a solution.

During the first lecture of my training, the teacher said –"When you tell people you practise hypnotherapy you will get strange looks and questions".

He was right.

If I am asked what work I do, I reply "I am a therapist using hypnosis".

There is often a pause, as if the questioner doesn't know what to say. This pause is followed by questions such as –"Are you like Paul McKenna?"; "Could you hypnotise me now?", "What happens if they don't wake up?" and the most incomprehensible of them all, "Does it work?"

I answer the last question with a single word—"No." This tends to bring our conversation to an abrupt halt!

Our clients can learn to resolve their problems by many different therapeutic methods, but the one I find the most successful is for them to have a positive personal experience following a consultation. When the client has such an experience, they move out of the world of theory and into the world of knowing the therapy has worked.

This book is written by therapists who have that experience. They have practised for many years and know what works, how to do things, where to find information—that is why we can trust their advice and learn from their experience.

They write about specific subjects essential for hypnotherapeutic practice—the "what to do", and "how to do" of therapy. They share their experience gleaned over many years, learned from things that worked and those that didn't.

I remember, many years ago, being enthralled by all the wisdom that other people seem to have, and I didn't.

I have a tendency to ask unusual (inane) questions and asked a tutor how I could become wise. He replied, "You can't become wise until you are old."

I am old now, but I am not sure I have become wise!

I don't know the ages of the authors of this book, but in my opinion they have achieved wisdom and are sharing it with you. Perhaps their words will help you find a quicker way to find wisdom than growing old!

Beginning at the beginning

The book is set out in specific chapters, each covering a subject important for the practise of hypnotherapy.

It begins at the beginning.

I remember when I started practising hypnosis I attended a seminar entitled: "Who cares for the carer!"

I was not sure how that would be of help, but during that day I realized how important it is to look after oneself, and since then I have remembered to be aware of my needs, alongside those of my clients.

Long ago I was drained of all my energy by a client I would describe as "an emotional vampire".

His manner, behavior, attitude and words were all extremely negative.

After the session I found myself completely exhausted and barely able to get out of my chair.

I thought long and hard about whether I should continue my practise if I was going to be so affected by negative clients.

In some strange way that experience taught me to protect myself, look after myself, and still be able to help clients. I have seen many similar clients since then, but have not been affected as I was. I don't know how I did it, but I believe my instinct was warning me to be wary when such clients attended.

The first chapter by Ann Jaloba is about looking after yourself, having time for yourself and not giving everything for your clients' needs.

She gives advice about many aspects of practice --- how to be the best therapist you can be; utilising supervision; time management and learning what aspect of therapy you wish to make your specialty.

The next chapter illustrates how old I am, and how things have changed since I started being a therapist. It is about marketing.

I was a G.P and anaesthetist (and played professional Australian football in my spare time!) when I became enthralled with hypnosis.

In those days of long ago doctors were not allowed to advertise. They would be struck off the register if they did.

I was lucky because I could see patients as a G.P, and if appropriate could suggest they see me for hypnosis.

I even delivered my patients' babies and used hypnosis at the same time for analgesia!

Marketing or advertising are very foreign to me. The word 'marketing' has a similar effect as 'the plague'.

So I was very interested in the chapter on marketing by Nic Griffiths and Debs Pearce. I realize how difficult it must be to acquire clients (if you are not a G.P, anesthetist and footballer!).

They have such helpful advice on the subject of marketing.

There are so many options; so much money can be spent (wasted); so many promises advertised, that it is essential you make use of the expert help Nic and Debs are offering.

My advice is to read the marketing chapter very carefully and note how it could fit in with the needs of your practice.

Our own experience
Most of our clients are worriers, and need to be reassured about their symptoms and their future! Whatever problems cause clients to seek our help; fear, worry and anxiety will be in the

background, either causing the problem, or worrying about the symptom.

Fiona Nicolson has given anxiety the priority it deserves in the first of the therapeutic chapters.

She describes both general and specific anxieties, how they affect the client, calibrations, symptoms, and how to treat them.

She explains in detail a number of approaches for treating anxious clients, session by session and provides a case history to illustrate the methods she uses.

When people are asked what conditions they associate with hypnosis, the most common response is —"Smoking and weight loss".

Cathy Simmons and Steve Miller have covered these two subjects as experts. They have both 'been there' —Cathy as a smoker and Steve having been overweight.

Cathy sought help on many occasions but the effects were always temporary. When she eventually did stop, she explored why this had occurred, and found a method that works. She has since become an expert on addictions, treating smokers is one of them.

She has carefully analysed the many components of smoking and stopping smoking; the character of the smoker, triggers, and systems involved, memory, reprogramming the mind and many more.

She provides a step by step process for anyone seeing smokers, and 'gives away' many of the methods she created to be successful in this area.

Steve Miller's approach to weight reduction is similar and different to Cathy's. He is more assertiveand uses what he calls the "A,B,C" framework of therapy; Attitude, Behaviors, and Capability.

Steve uses a variety of techniques to guide clients to eat in a way that will help lose weight and still be nourished.

I am aware of the difficulties he may have, as I ran a weight loss clinic for six years and found it very difficult to help clients lose weight and keep it off.

His therapy has hypnosis as a mainstay of treatment, and describes the different forms of hypnotherapy that suit his needs.

He is very straight talking and goes through the six sessions that are the mainstay of his treatment.

Anyone wishing to specialise in stopping smoking or weight loss should surely have these chapters at hand.

Helping clients have more choices
Here I would like to add a comment from my own experience. Some years ago I read a saying that has remained in my mind.

It is "People do the best they can with the choices they have. The aim of therapy is to help them have more choices."

I find that a helpful framework when seeing clients who are stuck, not progressing and losing heart.

As the sessions progress I rack my brain trying to help them make a change, any change, that may create another choice.

Often the change is hampered by the desire to stay the same.

There are two forces—often opposing. One is the belief people have; the other is the rational fact about the situation. I will illustrate what I mean with a brief case history.

Liz was 20 years old and terrified of going on a bus with doors that closed.

I saw her for a few sessions and she made good progress. I asked her to go on a bus for one stop, and let me know what she learnt from this.

I saw her two weeks later and she said she has been on a bus for six stops.

I congratulated her, and said she must be feeling very proud of herself.

She replied: "No. It was a Sunday and that doesn't count!"

Pat Duckworth writes about phobias, a very important condition for hypnotherapists as it responds well to hypnotherapy.

Pat also describes how other therapies such as NLP are very helpful with this condition. This highlights how we should all have a number of therapies under our control so we don't just have one string to our bow.

Pat writes eloquently and thoroughly about phobias. She takes you through every step of the way—the definition of phobias and how they are caused; symptoms; a questionnaire; future pacing; the Fast Phobia Cure of NLP; the contents of each session, and much more.

Her writing is very easy to follow and she provides many alternatives for therapy whatever the cause or symptoms.

It is important to know the person as well as the symptom. In life it is not only what people say, but who says it.

In my experience phobias may be relatively easy to help, but this depends on the character, beliefs and attitude of the client.

Many years ago I was rung by a man who asked if I would see his wife who had a phobia of slugs.

I said I would and a few weeks later met them at my practice.

The husband asked if he could see me first, and explained that his wife had feared slugs for years. Recently they attended a formal dinner and his wife was in conversation with the man next to her. He remarked he had put his gardening boots on that morning, and had squashed two slugs residing in them.

His wife got such a shock she stood up in horror, knocking food all over the table and the other guests.

That is why he brought her to see me.

He added as he left the room, "On no account must you mention the word 'slug,' or my wife will walk out!"

I can't remember how I handled this situation; I do recall being at a loss for words being forbidden to mention the 'S' word, but in the end—after some considerable time- I was able to help her with her phobia.

I wish I had read Pat's chapter all those years ago, although I did not find any reference to slugs.

Clem Turners Overview of Pain is what he says—an overview.

He includes many different aspects of pain management, not only hypnotherapy, and describes the many varieties of pain that we can suffer. He also lists the multitude of treatments that are available, from NLP to HCBT.

He writes about the different ways clients can alter their lifestyle to help their pain.

He describes hypnotherapy sessions, and how these can be tailored to individual needs, and blockages that can get in the way of treatment. Unlike phobias, pain management can be very difficult, and knowledge and experience such as Clem has are invaluable.

I know very little about the treatment of Irritable Bowel Syndrome, apart from the work of Professor Whorwell in Manchester, who put hypnosis on the 'medical map' for treatment of IBS.

Debbie Waller's chapter on Irritable Bowel Syndrome is like a thesis on this condition.

I think everything you need to know about IBS and its treatment, are in the pages of chapter eight.

Debbie emphasizes the importance of treating each patient as an individual, rather than treating the disease.

She even includes a script used by an IBS sufferer-Duncan Murray- who has devised this script specifically for IBS clients.

What Milton Erickson said to me

To finish my Foreword I would like to tell you a story with a message.

In 1979 I visited Dr. Milton Erickson in Phoenix Arizona to

attend a brief workshop. During the workshop he told all the students he would like them to climb a small mountain called Squaw Peak the following morning.

He said: "When you climb Squaw Peak you will find something very important about yourself."

The next morning a few students and I started climbing the mountain. After half an hour I realised I was lagging behind the others and thought, "I had better hurry and catch up with them."

Then I thought: "Why hurry, it doesn't matter, go at your own pace, do it your way."

And I did!

And I have been doing things my own way ever since. I have made many mistakes and learnt from them, but I have felt free to be myself. I believe even though the situation in Arizona was very trivial, the thought I had on the mountain made a major change in my attitude and has served me well ever since.

One of my concerns about clients is that their lives are run by what I call "The English Disease" or "What will people think?"

I do hope you learn to feel good about yourself, run your practice as you wish to, choose special conditions to treat that you have an instinct for; and learn from others and books like this one.

Now you have learnt what I learnt, without having to go to all the trouble of climbing Squaw Peak!

I do look forward to "The Hypnotherapy Handbook Number Two".

Brian Roet is a medical doctor from Melbourne. He came to London for a three month holiday 30 years ago and has stayed (not for the weather or beaches!).

He has written a number of books on hypnotherapy and associated subjects such as Confidence and Feelings.

He enjoys puzzles and regards the client's symptoms as a

puzzle. His aim is to help the client solve their own puzzle by helping them "see what they can't see".

He believes self-confidence (or the lack of it) is a major factor in the problems of clients and thinks one of the major skills in therapy is attentive listening.

He runs workshops on a variety of subjects including "Integrated Parts Therapy—finding the Metaphors and Symbols that Cause Symptoms".

His website is www.brianroet.co.uk

Chapter One

Taking care of yourself

Looking after yourself and getting the basics in place is essential if you want your new career to get off to a good start. Ann Jaloba runs through what you should do to get off to the best professional start you can.

I always remember a story a very successful therapist told me. He'd had a good solid career in a large organisation, but it didn't satisfy him and he had decided to become a full-time hypnotherapist. He trained with a well-known school and found the training fulfilling and fascinating. He was paying attention right from the beginning to the need to build a client list and develop a business.

By the time he had finished his training, everything was in place and he felt the decision to become a hypnotherapist was the right decision for him, he knew he had the skills to make a difference and to build a good practice.

The day came when he handed in his notice at the large corporate organisation where he had worked for 20 years, the leaving party was held and he was waving goodbye for the last time. And, he had to admit he was terrified.

He remembers looking in the rear view mirror of his car as he left for good and seeing his old corporate headquarters disappearing into the distance when it suddenly hit him that he was on his own now. If he didn't do lots of things he would have no clients, no income and no career. He had known this intellectually and had prepared, but the emotional impact caught him unawares.

The emphasis was on now on him – it was down to him and him alone.

Relying on yourself

I'm sure most of us have felt something similar, it might even be the thing which is holding you back. Perhaps you feel you have a lot to offer, but that becoming an independent professional is too daunting.

It's easy to see why so many people who train in our profession feel like this. You have to be so grown up don't you? There is no leaning on your workmates when there is trouble. You cannot turn to corporate rules and procedures to guide you through a difficult time. It can be hard to take time off, even if you are feeling unwell.

Sometimes family and friends imagine that you have lots of spare time because you are not going to someone else's office every day and you will have to risk upsetting them when you explain you cannot spend an hour on the phone every morning. And then you may have a nagging fear . . .what if it all goes wrong. You may feel that if this happens have only yourself to blame – and us therapists are so very good at blaming ourselves.

When you think about it, it's no wonder many of us find this transition from corporate person to independent professional difficult.

Many possibilities

But it is worth making that transition and not just for you. The world needs more good therapists and if you can make the leap you will find yourself in one of the most rewarding professions there is. We live in a world where insecurity and loneliness is ubiquitous and unhappiness is rife, yet at the same time people are more aware of their need to look after their mental health and well-being. It is a very good time to develop a therapy career, there is the need and there is the opportunity.

Yet most therapists who train do not manage to make a full-time career in therapy. For some, this is an active choice, but others find themselves unable to attract enough clients, or find themselves burning out as they find the challenge of keeping boundaries between work and personal life too much.

Perhaps one of the main problems is, at the start of our new career, we are so busy focussing on growing our business that we neglect to give proper space and respect to the need to change and prepare ourselves for what is a major turn in our lives. Moving into this profession can be as big a life change as moving house or having a child, so don't underestimate the need to plan, prepare and take care of yourself. It can be done, it can be fun, but you do need to be flexible, reflective and resilient.

Benefits for you

I am going to give some guidance as to how to do this. The smoother you can make the transition into a competent independent professional, the better therapist you will be.

And think of all the benefits to you if you do make it. The satisfaction you will gain by putting your hard-won training into practice.

By choosing this career, you can determine what you do, what you specialise in, who you see, when you work and how you work. And then you help people; they arrive miserable and go away happier – what could be better than that? That freedom and that sense of satisfaction can make work seem like fun – and it's hard to imagine a more worthwhile life choice.

So what do you need to do to get your mind in the right place to be a good independent practitioner? I think a few words sum it up: boundaries, planning, support, and learning. Get those in place and you will be okay.

Easy isn't it? Well that depends, look at yourself as if you were a client. What would you say to a client who wanted to do something but was stuck? I bet it would be something like: "You've got to be willing to change what you do." "Change can feel difficult at first, but it is worth it." You are used to these ideas; you use them with your clients and know how effective they can be. You know many techniques for helping clients make the sorts of changes they need to make and they can apply to you as well. You deserve to give yourself sufficient time to make the changes you will need to make if your new career is to be successful.

Start with the vision

Start with yourself, how are you going to be in the world now you are embarking on this new career? Take every aspect of yourself and use all your senses to develop a very strong sense and vision of this professional self. How will you look, what will you wear, how will your workspace be, what will your clients think of you? Future pace how this is going to be for you. Ask yourself what achievements you will be most proud of in a year's time. How will that change your life? How will you celebrate these achievements?

Then do what neuro linguistic programmers would call an ecology check: how does this 'new you' fit in with your family, your friends, your clients, actual and potential, your professional friends and networks. You can then begin to establish how your new professional plans fit in with your wider life. You will know where you will draw your main support from. It helps if you have the full backing of your family as your new role is likely to mean changes to your domestic routine. Support from friends is important, although you might find some people misunderstand what you are doing; they may even feel threatened as you step out of your familiar patterns. So be prepared to explain how you are going to be working, when you have time and when you are not available.

Your new role is going to stretch your skills in many different areas. You know yourself well, so you can anticipate what will be easy for you and what might prove more difficult. You might want to consider what parts of your new professional life you are going to be good at and what areas you may need help with. If you are bad at managing money, for example, as I am, then you need to find yourself a good accountant, as I did.

This might sound obvious, but as an independent professional you will find you have to deal with areas which previously have been someone else's responsibility. Take some time and list what challenges you will face and how you will deal with them. Don't be afraid to seek help for the things which are not the core part of your business, which is delivering therapy. You do not want to be spending time on essential but extraneous parts of your business; getting professional help can save you time and effort and that time and effort can go into delivering a service to your clients.

Boundaries can free you

Boundaries do not need to fence you in, rather they can protect you and allow you a protected space in which you can develop, learn new things, be creative and even take a few risks.

As you begin to get a sense of yourself in your new professional space, you will get a sense of where work ends and your personal life begins, developing a sense of what the boundaries of this space are and what feels right for you. This is important, once you feel comfortable and familiar with who you are professionally then you can decide how this professional you fits with your personal life.

Use what you know

As a therapist, you will probably have come across how important this is in your interventions with clients. Clients who are stressed, for example, have often lost the sense of a boundary between their personal and professional life; it can be that worries about work infect every area of their lives to the detriment of their well being.

Working as a therapist, getting those strong boundaries is just as important for you. In fact, it is even more important in this type of work. You will be giving a lot of yourself emotionally at work as you are dealing with people's personal lives. In addition, you may be working from home and this can add to difficulty of putting those boundaries in place.

Conscious planning before you start can really help here. One way of doing this is to think about your whole day and the natural breaks within it.

Use these natural breaks to mark out your personal time throughout the day. Develop little rituals to tell yourself 'my time'. This can be something as simple as drinking from a special cup or taking a short break in the garden; what you choose will be right for you.

You might also consider how you are going to mark the end of your working day – even if this end of day just means leaving your home office to walk to the kitchen, make it a little occasion; just as if you were leaving your old city building to get the tube home. Perhaps taking five minutes to reflect on how you feel the day went and a setting aside a defined period and space to relax before you do other things works for you. I use this time to keep a reflective diary and assess and learn from what has happened in the day. You will decide what fits for you, the key thing is making space and time to consider this, otherwise you are in danger of allowing your work time to take over your whole life. Then you will never truly rest and will become burned out.

Discipline yourself in a way which feels congruent with your personality.

This doesn't mean telling yourself off, and we therapists tend to be very good at being hard on ourselves. Real discipline is being kind to yourself as it helps you work with the flow of your personality.

A good plan is to decide on what you will do and focus until you have done it. Make a daily plan and work through it. Take defined breaks for yourself and work when you are not on those breaks. Know your own patterns and energy flows and work with them. This way you will get more done and be aware of those natural breaks, take time out to congratulate yourself on what you have achieved at this point as this can be an energy boost as well.

Use your professional image to support you

How you look and present yourself and how you arrange and present your work space is central to the development of your professional self.

You are not only sending your clients a message about your values and attitudes, you are sending this message to yourself as well. When you walk into your workspace take the chance to feel the difference, you are now entering professional mode and let that rush of confidence and control take over. If you feel this, you will communicate it to your clients and you are much more likely to have successful outcomes. You will be sending out the right sort of signals to help clients rely upon you and trust you.

entation and image

Your own presentation and image can, if you get it right, not only benefit your business building it can make you feel right about yourself as a professional. Your clients will want to know you are the type of person who can run their own life well, so looking good and being in a work space which looks good will build their confidence in you and your confidence in yourself.

Getting your work space right for you can give you a huge psychological benefit; helping you feel confident about yourself. Knowing exactly how is it to be in professional mode means you can identify easily when you leave it.

This means you are in a good mental place to then begin to put into place those boundaries which you will need if you are to keep your energy levels flowing. If you have this professional mode going strong you will find it easy and natural to decide on such things as when to answer your work phone and how many days to take off every week.

Professional mode is the right place to start imagining in detail what you want from your new career. Do this using the modalities which are right for you and do it in detail, the greater richness you can get into the future you are imagining the more powerful that vision will be.

Focus on that you want

Also, by putting in the detail you will begin to get a much stronger feeling about what really matters to you, as you imagine begin to ask what feels good, what really excites you about your goals. Focus on those things, how can you do the maximum of these things and less of the things you find less interesting. The detailed imagining can also do something else for you; it can show you what your pinch points are – these can come at you from various angles. So as you imagine, does some area about your work feel 'not quite right' – this might encourage you to think about why.

A discussion with peers or your supervisor might be a good move here (more of this later).

As you reflect you might ask, is this 'not quite right' coming from a lack of confidence: does this mean you need more skills, or do you often underestimate what you have to give, if so how can you change this? Or the 'not quite right' could be you telling yourself that you are not a good fit with a particular aspect of your work.

Flexibility and support

This can be a great starting point for planning and goal setting. Again, use the skills you would use with your clients. Set realistic goals and map out your path to reach them, and then regularly record how you are doing.

Be flexible, some things will work better than others and some things will surprise you. We all tend to get stuck in ways of thinking and being, so being truly flexible means turning to others for support for nearly all of us.

Don't underestimate the need to do this. An estimated 60 percent of new therapists stop practising within two years and frequently cite burnout as a cause. Signs of burnout include feelings of exhaustion, loss of appetite, lowered immunity and a feeling of hopelessness. Burnout affects people in many different careers, but therapists seems to be particularly at risk because of the intense emotional work they are involved in. So protecting yourself is important.

Growing through supervision

This is where supervision comes in. Many people get allergic when they hear the word, they imagine being monitored, judged and criticised; but good supervision is the opposite of this. As a qualified supervisor for the National Council for Hypnotherapy, I am constantly delighted at how much I learn from my supervisees and how they grow and develop in our sessions.

In supervision sessions, my supervisees get a chance to review and reflect on their work in order to do it better. This is a creative, supportive process which is energising and fun.

A supervisee who is reflecting on his or her practice will, under skilled questioning in a supervision session, find they have the knowledge and resources to deliver therapy to clients and to better appreciate the support they might need to continue to improve their work as a therapist.

I always ask supervisees: "what did you learn about yourself?" This can be very enlightening, when you are new it can be difficult to conceptualise your cases as you don't have your own body of work to inform you and your decision making. Get yourself a good supervisor and you can tap into their experience, it can be very comforting to have a space to develop ideas with someone who has been there before. Use this space to explore your own reactions and choices and enjoy developing your confidence and competence.

You will find if you are in a good supervisory relationship then it is with you all the time, not just when you are in session with your supervisor.

You will find yourself developing the mental habits of noting your emotional reactions to clients, of considering the different possibilities for intervention, of knowing how to measure your success with clients.

As a practising therapist you are now learning by doing – your actions matter and every client intervention can be a chance for you to develop.

Using you time well

It is unlikely when you are just starting out that you will have a full client list. This means you will have quiet times, and there will be times when you ask if you have made the right decision to go into this business.

At these times it is even more important to make clear boundaries and use your time well. When I look back to my first few months in business, I am glad I was not too busy. The extra time allowed me to put together packs of high quality information on the areas in which I wanted to specialise, some of these still form the basis of the material I give to clients today. I also used this time to develop the reflective diary I still keep and to build up local networks of colleagues, many of whom I still see.

Make sure you do not panic yourself into forgetting your boundaries. It is all too easy if you don't have any clients to start answering the telephone at any hour of the day or night or to find yourself giving long telephone consultations for free in the hope of getting that next client.

Use your quiet time to set yourself some rules which feel comfortable for you. I try to limit telephone calls with potential clients to 10 minutes and I only answer my phone within certain hours.

Picking your clients and finding your niche

Many successful therapists build a niche business. Becoming a real expert in one field can really pay off. Some people decide which areas they wish to focus on very early in the career, sometimes while they are still training. Do not be afraid of acknowledging and using your previous life experience to build your career. One colleague whom I supervise specialises in weight loss, she became a hypnotherapist after a good experience using hypnotherapy to lose weight. She is very open in her publicity about her struggles and ultimate success in reaching a healthy weight and this 'I've been there' approach attracts clients to her. Her passion and her conviction of the efficacy of hypnotherapy shines through and gives her clients confidence.

For others it takes a bit longer to decide the area in which you can be of most help. Keep good notes and a reflective diary and certain patterns will begin to emerge.

Reflection and learning

I make time at the end of each working day to fill out a reflective diary. It is very simple in form, I have certain headings: detail of the activity I am reflecting upon; any aspect of this which caused me concern; what I learned from the activity; anything I would do differently in the future. Filling this out every working day has become a habit for me and something I find immensely useful at many levels. The process of taking time, making a quiet, secure space where I can honestly assess how well I have helped my clients helps me. Filling out my diary marks the end of the working day for me, once I have completed this, I can concentrate on my personal life and put work away for the evening.

I also use my reflective diary as the basis for my regular sessions with my supervisor.

Reading it back every few weeks helps me get a perspective on how things are going and helps me see any patterns developing. I can spot any areas where perhaps I am 'stuck'; I can ask myself if I am relying too much on a certain type of intervention, for example. I might notice I am feeling rather tired, I can use my diary to ask if I have a run of particularly demanding clients, or perhaps I am seeing too many clients at the moment.

You may find over time that you enjoy dealing with certain issues more than others, you may also find you enjoy seeing certain types of people. Be slightly careful when you are starting out, most of us have a tendency to prefer treating people like us and this can limit you unnecessarily. However, most of us will find that it is easier to build rapport with certain personality types or people with certain outlooks and beliefs and there is nothing wrong with this.

Trust your own judgement and feel free to verbalise how you feel to your supervisor or your professional network. You will find that trusting your instincts will help you become a happy confident practitioner; you will communicate that good mental state to your clients and that will give them the feeling that you are the sort of person they would like to see.

If you build a good rapport you are much more likely to have a successful outcome. This is what you want at every level: you will build your reputation and therefore get more business, you will get the satisfaction of helping another person, you will build your knowledge and competence in the most positive way.

Continuing Professional Development

If you build a niche you will also find you can use your professional development time and budget more effectively. And continuing professional development is essential to looking after yourself.

Most people think of courses when they think of continuing professional development. Courses are great, you can learn a lot in a short time and meet other people with the same interests as you, so there is lots going for them. But continuing professional development can be many other things and you can be very creative and very flexible in what you do. So reading books and articles, attending webinars, going to networking groups can all help your development. If you have decided to niche you can use all these to build up and expertise.

Professional organisations

You may be wondering where to access the best continuing professional development. One good way is through a joining a professional organisation.

One word of warning here, anyone can set up a professional organisation so you could end up spending money on an organisation which does not have the members, infrastructure or knowledge to offer a good service. So it is worth asking how many members an organisation has, what professional qualifications and experience its officers have, and what its ethical and complaints procedures are. Another good check (if you are in the United Kingdom) is if the organisation is a member of the Complementary and Natural Healthcare Council (CNHC). (The CNHC was set up with government support to protect the public by providing a UK voluntary register of complementary therapists. CNHC's register has been approved as an Accredited Voluntary Register by the Professional Standards Authority for Health and Social Care.)

To join the CNHC, a professional organisation needs to adhere to strict ethical and professional standards. If you have this protection, you not only have a professional resource to help you, you also have another way of showing your clients that you are a serious professional who takes their welfare and protection seriously.

You are not alone

I hope I have given you enough pointers to ensure that you feel supported and can protect yourself as you develop as a therapist.

There is a lot of help and support out there and it is quite easy to build up a network of fellow professionals.

With a background in health journalism, Ann was deputy editor of Nursing Standard; *she also managed the website of the Royal College of Nursing. She became interested in hypnotherapy while running a charity website which offered online support to women with breast cancer. She is now is an author, editor, trainer, supervisor and hypnotherapy practitioner. She has recently written* FIRSTdays: how to set up a therapy business and stay sane, *to help people have a successful first year in a therapy business. She edits* The Hypnotherapy Journal, *the quarterly journal of the National Council for Hypnotherapy. She runs training courses in setting up a successful business; in using hypnotherapy to manage workplace anxiety; in hypnotherapy and weightloss and in writing books for publication. She trained with the Academy of Clinical and Medical Hypnosis and has a busy practice in Sheffield.*

Ann is an NCH Accredited Hypnotherapy Supervisor and a founder of SupervisionPlus, an organisation which offers its members high quality supervision, plus regular webinars and a private online networking and support service.

Ann is currently writing a Guide to Managing Workplace Stress.

See more about Ann at www.wellthought.co.uk or contact her for supervision at www.supervisionplus.org

Chapter Two

Marketing your new business

Do You Want More Clients? Nic Griffiths and Debs Pearce are hypnotherapists with very successful practices. Here they share their experience of how marketing well can build a successful business and how, with a targeted approach, you can build a thriving practice.

It has to be borne in mind that many therapists either don't like marketing or don't understand it. It might therefore be helpful to contemplate Nic's mantra: If you don't market yourself correctly then your potential clients won't know you're there. Therefore the likelihood is that you won't be successful and at some point you may have to get another job to pay the bills. At that job you will have a boss who will give you something to do that you either don't like or you don't understand! At least by getting to grips with marketing, it will allow you to carry on practising your therapy, which is something you really want to do.

When launching a business, it is not unrealistic to expect a person to spend five, six or even seven hours a week on their marketing activity – possibly more. As time goes by referrals will gradually build and help sustain or increase your business further. You may want to bear in mind that to sustain a full-time business on referrals alone, you'll need to see a huge number of clients! You need to do a lot of work in the early years of your business to get to this level and you'll need to spend at least a couple of hours a week working on your marketing. Once you have built this momentum, you still need to continue – you never know when it might go quiet, so the marketing engine should be chugging away in the background keeping that flow of clients coming through your door.

What exactly is marketing?

Marketing is simply a collective term for a range of activities, including:

• Advertising – usually paid for and appearing in many forms such as newspaper adverts and online campaigns, such as Google AdWords.

• Public Relations (PR) – this is generally free activity ranging from press releases and articles you submit to local publications through to word of mouth. You can be undertaking some PR activity simply by talking to an existing client and inspiring them!

• Branding – how you look, what your photo says about you, how your business portrays itself.

• Plus loads more for bigger businesses, but we're going to keep it simple here!

Marketing takes time, effort and energy and it's a mistake to simply focus on one avenue of marketing. Don't just think about what you like, you need to put yourself in your clients' shoes. In order to attract the maximum number of clients and for your business to be successful, you need to consider all avenues of marketing activity. You don't need to do this all at once; a step by step approach is just fine.

Where to start?

It always pays to have a plan. We don't mean you need to have a detailed plan, a rough idea of what you want to achieve will be fine. Here are some of the things it's useful to think about:
- What do you do? How do your clients benefit from your service?
- What is good about you, what's your Unique Selling Proposition (USP)?
- What are your main objectives? How are you going to achieve them? (Action point lists are always good.)
- Who are your potential clients, for example, are they within a certain age range or demographic that may sway where or how you market yourself?
- Where are your potential clients, where are they looking and what do they want?

It is then useful to ask, how many clients you want? Check if there are any deadlines you must stick to and put them in your calendar. Then make a note of any key tasks you want to achieve. Last but not least, work out how much this is going to cost and if it is within your budget.
Good websites that might help you to start planning are:
www.gov.uk/starting-up-a-business and
www.businessballs.com

Get inspired – get clients

Let's make marketing easier. Talk to fellow therapists, not just therapists in your field, but any sort and see what works for them. It can be quite inspiring to talk to any self-employed person to exchange ideas and it's certainly a way of motivating yourself. Being self-employed, especially as a therapist, can be an isolating career even if you work in a clinic, so getting that interaction is important.

If you talk to other therapists and especially if you do reciprocal treatments, we know from personal experience that you WILL get referrals. Who would have thought that sitting down with a therapist over a cup of tea was marketing?

People are different, so you need different styles of marketing

When attracting new clients, it's good to remember that not all clients are the same. Take time to consider your potential clients and what they will be looking for – do not fall into the trap of thinking they will track you down in the same way you would track yourself down!

There are different models of car for good reason; there are even different colour cars, why? Because people like different things. The wider your appeal, the more clients you will get. Clients look for what they want/need in different ways.

So often we hear people say, "Don't advertise in the paper – these days it's much better to advertise on the Internet". Well to a degree they are right, it's very important to have a presence on the web, but your general branding should be out there for all to see even when they're not looking for you. Why are perfumes advertised in national magazines as well as TV? Because people do still pick up newspapers and magazines.

Both of us advertise every month in local magazines, even parish magazines, as well as the Internet. We only advertise in the local newspapers for special occasions or to encourage the papers to publish our press releases (more on this later). We cast our net wide to capture the maximum amount of exposure.

Drip feeding is a key aspect to successful marketing!

It's much better to 'drip feed' than do one big splash. Nic had a daily national newspaper do three major stories on her hypnotherapy business, yet as she recalls, she didn't get one piece of 'paying' business from those stories.

Her phone rang a lot, but the enquiries were from all around the country and therefore not suitable for her locality. Yet Nic's little advert in a local magazine that goes to 12,000 residents in her town pulls in 3-4 clients per month on average, but some months she won't get anything from it.

It's the drip feed that's important.

Think about those big advertisers like BMW and Coca-Cola, why do they repeatedly advertise? It's because they need to build that background awareness and so do you. It's also vital to get your message out there in more than one way to build a successful business.

The national newspaper's coverage of Nic's business wasn't a total waste of time though, it gave valuable exposure for her business that she was able to utilise.

Although the newspaper would have hit most bins by the following day, in Nic's clinic there's a copy of that article on the wall to act as good PR!

Stationery is also marketing!

Letterheads
Your letterhead should contain your logo and contact details. It should have a professional feel given you may be sending correspondence to companies and clients alike at some point. You also find yourself corresponding with someone in the medical profession.

If you feel you'll only use letterheads occasionally, there is nothing wrong with simply getting a logo designed and then producing your own letterhead as a template Word document. You can then print your letters straight onto your letterhead template.

Remember to check out printing costs if you want to get them professionally printed – instant print companies versus your local printer (if you build up a professional relationship with locals, they might even introduce business to you in the future, so it's not all about costs!).

Business cards

These wonderfully convenient cards advertise your logo and contact details.

These days it is common to expand your marketing by printing on the reverse of the card, for example conditions you can help or maybe different clinics you practise in.

Think of the back of your business card as an advert for your business.

Business cards can be a useful *aide memoire*, so hand them out whenever you can. Always carry them on you as you never know who you might bump into.

Debs always includes a couple of business cards in therapy-related correspondence she sends out, with the belief that the person receiving them will hand them onto others.

Branding. This means YOU!

Branding covers a number of elements: including how you portray yourself, for example your photo; your logo and design of your marketing on your leaflets and adverts; Your branding also includes You!! You are your branding when you are a self-employed therapist. Take some time to consider who you are, what you do and who your likely clients are going to be?

Your Photo

Above all it should be professional. Your photo makes a statement that you mean business. We'd recommend you engage a professional photographer, which is likely to cost anywhere between £70 and £150. It's an investment well worth making.

Your photo should be warm, a smile is always good – remember you're starting the therapeutic alliance right here. So imagine someone stood behind the cameraman whilst your photo is being taken, someone with Mickey Mouse ears perhaps or maybe the Vicar of Dibley.

Think of something funny, such as your favourite comedian and what would be happening if they were standing behind the camera. Your photo is a huge marketing tool that if used correctly will make the difference between a client coming to you or your competition.

Don't be tempted to use a holiday or wedding snap, just because you happen to be looking your best.

Watch out for the background, make sure it's suitable before you start – take a few test shots. Also, remember you need a high resolution version for printed material such as leaflets, and a low resolution version for your website, otherwise it'll slow down the pages when they're loading.

Your photo is a large part of your business, it should appear everywhere possible: your website, your leaflets, your adverts. The more your photo appears, the more you get known and the more clients you are likely to get!

We both agree that we absolutely hate having our photo taken, but it is truly worth the pain – honestly! This is the first step to building the therapeutic alliance with your client. Some research advises that the therapeutic alliance is more important than the therapy itself, so do realise this is a very important part of your marketing.

Your Logo

You should consider the following when having your logo designed:

1. Who is your audience, is it the general public or are you more likely to be appealing to the corporate market? This should be conveyed to the person designing your logo.
2. What do you want to convey with your logo – relaxation, healing, change of mindset, strength or something else?
3. When you look at the options your designer gives you, consider whether they 'fit' with your business and how you will appear to your clients. For instance, if your logo is sharp and strong, it might appeal to the corporate sector, if it's gentle and calming it might appeal to females.

You don't want your branding to give the impression of being one type of therapist and then when the client arrives they are surprised to find you are not what they expected.

Leaflets

One of the key aspects of your marketing is your leaflet. Your leaflet should complement your stationery and website and you may be surprised at how many you will use up if you're using them correctly.

Your main leaflet should be used in response to general enquiries, displayed in clinics, used at promotional events, given out to whoever will take them! Both of us give one to every new client even if they already have one – you never know who they may know!

Your leaflet should be concise and clear. Ideally you will need one generic leaflet covering your services, but remember to keep it well structured and clear – if you overload it with too much information you are in danger of confusing your client.

A good tip here is to put yourself in your clients' shoes. What are they looking for help with? And what is your answer to their problem? Your answers could form your main headlines, with explanations on how you can help.

Have a small section on who you are and your qualifications which, ideally, should be towards the end of the leaflet followed by your contact details.

Maybe refer them to your website for your prices so that the leaflet doesn't date should you need to change them. Your website should be your main portal of information, your leaflet is a general guide which also signposts to your website for further information. Getting hold of a few of your competitors' leaflets may help you decide on what you want to say.

Leaflets come in all shapes and sizes, but a good choice is an A4 leaflet that folds to 1/3 A4. This neatly fits in a standard DL envelope and into most clinic display units. It should be light, appealing and not crammed for space.

Photography

The photography in your marketing material is important. Use online photo libraries where you can download images if you want, but make sure you've purchased the images as the fines for using unauthorised pictures run into many thousands! As we have already seen, it really does help if you have a photo of yourself in your marketing and that includes your brochure. It begins the therapeutic alliance before the client even picks up the phone. Some people don't like having their photo taken but you have to understand that if you want more clients then this is a key way of getting them!

Printing

The higher the quantity you print initially, the lower the unit cost.

Therefore consider the lifespan of your leaflet and try to ensure that the content is reasonably generic and unlikely to change, so consider if you are likely to be changing your prices or your address. Once you have your design layout, obtain three different quotes with reasonable quality paper, so if possible see a sample of the paper beforehand as it will have an impact on the final result. In the UK at the time of writing this, VAT isn't applicable to leaflet printing, but do check!

Think about what you like when you pick up a brochure: what makes you look through it? Usually it's because it is relevant to you or because you like the look or feel of it. So not only is the headline on the front cover of vital importance, but so is the overall design and the quality of the paper.

Remember to keep it simple! What is your client looking for? If you try to come up with clever headlines, will your potential client understand what it is you do? A good way of checking whether you've got it right is to write out what you're thinking of doing on a piece of paper then show it to friends or relatives without saying a word. Ask them to tell you what message they think you're trying to get across. Don't get into a conversation about it as you won't be there when a potential client picks up your leaflet.

Bullet points are a very good way of getting information across fast, so do use them wherever you can.

Finally, double check spelling by reading the text backwards. Otherwise your brain will read what it 'wants' to read rather than what is there; reading backwards overcomes this!

Advertising

There are two schools of thought when it comes to whether advertising works: one school says that it doesn't work, the other says that it does.

Those who say it doesn't may have given up before the advertising has had chance to kick in. Advertising can be a slow burn activity and it can take some time before people respond to the call to action.

Both of us use advertising as part of our marketing mix. We like the fact that it's quick and easy to set up and we also like the certainty that we are getting our names out there.

The downside is that it can be costly.

Some people prefer to focus all of their marketing activity online. This can be very cost-effective, but it is sometimes time-consuming to get the adverts to work. It also does not reach those people in your potential client base who are not Internet savvy; there are still very many people who are more responsive to print media than online marketing. Some even feel the Internet is a transitory place, here today gone tomorrow, whereas when they see you in the press somehow it confirms you are here!

More traditional forms of advertising are having a resurgence as people can become fatigued with email overload, so it's a good idea to cover all bases, especially if you want to build a sturdy business and you need your branding to be strong.

Making the most of your budget

Here are a few tips to help you get the most from a small advertising budget:

Set aside some of your budget for online advertising, for example Google AdWords, this will ensure you have some guaranteed online visibility. Do bear in mind they have a different charging structure which you need to look into carefully so you're aware of the type of bill you're likely to get at the end of the month. Don't blow the remainder of your budget in one big advert, split it across a series of weekly/monthly smaller adverts.

The minimum size we would recommend is business-card size, any smaller and you won't look credible.

To begin with, concentrate on local publications that are distributed free, either displayed at local shops and businesses or preferably delivered door to door.

If you have a choice, go for higher-quality publications, such as small glossy publications, rather than cheap 'n' cheerful newspaper style, as the better quality magazines tend to stay around people's homes longer.

Local parish magazines represent excellent value for money and people *do* read them.

Paid-for newspaper circulation is in decline due to more people getting their news on-line, so only go this route if you've exhausted all the decent free publications.

Negotiate a good rate at the outset. When you're first presented with the costs (the 'rate card'), ask if that's the best they can do and what discount will you get if you commit to a series of adverts.

Maximising impact

Remember, the aim is for people to know you're there, so the more places they see you advertise and promote yourself the better. But it's better to go in the same publication for six months than it is to go in six publications for one month.

This is because it takes people a while to get around to taking action. Your first advert will arouse their interest. The second advert will remind them. The third and subsequent adverts usually start to generate those important leads.

It can be very tempting when trialling advertising to say; "I'll start by placing a single small advert and see how it goes." This is a waste of money.

Make sure your advert is going to be in an appropriate position in the publication – if they have a health and well-being section, this is ideal. When you first place an advert, get a commitment from the publication to allow you to have the occasional article published. Some publications offer 250-500 words of free editorial to therapists who advertise in the health and well-being section. They offer the space on a rota basis or on a first-come first-served basis. This gives extra credibility to your advertising and you should notice an increase in calls and hits to your website.

Keep it Local!

Most therapists we know provide an excellent service across a small geographic area. This provides an excellent opportunity for getting yourself known locally – you can soon become a kind of local celebrity. This applies even if you live in a city, although you have to be mindful to focus on local shops and organisations.

Buying locally
Having your photo in all your marketing material is a good start as it gets you recognised.

Then it's up to you to get out there and talk. If you're buying something for your therapy room, even if it's only cleaning materials or batteries for your clock, try to buy from small, local shops and be sure to drop the subject into the conversation. If the assistant expresses an interest, give them your business card (you *will* have them on you, won't you?).

Other therapists
Give reciprocal therapy sessions with other therapists in your clinic, if you work that way.

Some clinics hold 'swapsie' days when all the therapists get together and swap sessions. Once they know what your therapy is about they are more likely to recommend you. Make sure you have a supply of other therapists' cards from different disciplines so that you can make referrals, and make sure they have a supply of yours.

Giving talks and demos
Offer to give talks to local groups. If speaking in front of groups of people fills you with dread, offer to give them a live demonstration of your therapy – it's a little less daunting. Or you could offer reciprocal sessions with a hypnotherapist who could help you overcome your fear!

Hold an event
Get together with other therapists and hold an Open Day or Health & Well-Being event. Bear in mind that getting people to attend can be even more difficult than organising the event itself. A good tip is to run the event as a charity fund-raiser, so you could approach a local playgroup or hospice and offer to hold a pamper evening for their supporters.

Remember the purpose is to raise your profile, so be sure to issue press releases and take plenty of leaflets and business cards with you to the event.

You are a celebrity!
Aim to get to the point where everyone in the locality knows you are the local hypnotherapist. This means if they are in need of the kind of help you provide, you are front of their minds. They will come to you and this will build your business.

Public Relations (PR)

PR is a term used to describe activities that promote an organisation to its audience. PR activities differ from advertising in that they do not usually incur a cost (other than time and materials). In our case, it's about getting ourselves noticed by as many potential clients as possible.

PR is great if you have little or no budget, but it can be time consuming and sometimes the rewards are not always obvious or immediate. The value of PR is often longer term, it helps you raise awareness of your presence, it puts you on the map.

There is a whole raft of different activities that you can undertake:
- Giving talks.
- Running workshops.
- Holding Open Days.
- Attending Health & Well-being Fairs.
- Maintaining contact with clients.

Free Press Coverage

One of the most effective ways of generating awareness is by tapping into the local press.

Although we might imagine that the bigger the publication, the greater the impact, this isn't always the case. At our marketing company, TMS we have experienced good responses from small, local publications. It's almost as if people feel more comfortable with therapists who are close to them. Plus, of course, the smaller the publication the more likely they are to welcome additional material.

There are two main ways of getting yourself into local publications for free: issuing press releases and writing articles

Often the fact that you advertise in a publication will increase the likelihood of the publication including your story.

Press Release

What is a press release?
Put simply, it's a newsworthy story written in a format that

appeals to newspapers and other publications. So, have you done or are you about to do anything newsworthy? The chances are that you have, examples could be:
- Significant milestone: 100th client or three years in practice.
- Gaining a new qualification or skill.
- Attending a conference.
- Holding an Open Day.

If you live a very quiet life and you simply can't think of anything of interest, try tapping into national awareness days, like Asthma Awareness Week or Eating Disorders Awareness Week. Alternatively, produce something seasonal, such as 'de-stress in time for your holiday' or 'ease away aches and pains from gardening after the long winter'. As hypnotherapists we are lucky as the press frequently publishes good stories, so look out for these and see if you can rewrite them or refer to them.

Send the press release to as many local publications as you can think of. Larger publications will get hundreds each week, so it's a good idea to target smaller publications too.

Articles

Articles are generally more factual and less about news than press releases. A good idea is to ask your local publications for a features list. Most larger publications will pre-plan themes for certain times of the year, for example wedding season, holiday season or more specific topics such as mental well-being or mid-life career changes. Take a look at what features are coming up and see if you can write something relevant.

Alternatively you could write about something you feel comfortable with and then see if any local publications are interested. Your training course notes, or the hand-outs from a recent CPD event are a good source of inspiration and reference material.

You could of course add the material to your own website,

although you shouldn't do this if a publication has accepted your article as they will expect it to be exclusive to them. Also be careful you are not infringing anyone else's copyright, the material does need to be your own.

Websites

A website is an essential part of your marketing mix as the Internet is often the first place people look when they are seeking a service. If you haven't got a website you will be missing out on a huge market.

If you're not technically-minded, or you only have a small budget, all is not lost as there are plenty of free or low-cost ways to get a website up and running.
You will need:
• A website name (also known as a domain name or website address).
• The website itself (your web pages).
• A host environment or platform (a place for your website to 'live').

You will also want to ensure that your website appears towards the top of any search engine results, such as Google, when a potential customer searches online for your services. There are many ways to improve your position in the lists, and doing so is known as Search Engine Optimisation (SEO) – more of this later.

Your Website Name

If you haven't already decided on your website name, type it into a search engine, such as Google or Yahoo, and make sure you haven't got some major competitor with that name already, or possibly, some famous (or infamous) person of a similar name, who at the end of the day will be competing with you on search engines – and if they're that famous, you will lose the race!

You can easily check if the website name you require is available for you to buy. Simply log onto a site such as www.easily.co.uk or www.godaddy.com and search for what is available.

You can purchase your domain name with the click of a few buttons and a payment of between £5 and £20 for a two-year period depending on whether the address ends in .co.uk or a .com. Be wary – use a reputable company so that you're easily able to link your website name to your website.

You can have more than one domain name for your site, so you could purchase for instance, www.(yourname).co.uk and www.(yourname).com, or perhaps www.hypnosisforyou.com and www.hypnosis-cheltenham.co.uk. It's like having sign-posts around the outer ring road of a city, there's more than one directional sign to the city centre, similarly there can be more than one directional sign to your website!

Having the words relating to your service, such as your therapy type and your geographic location are good ways of coming up the search engine listings i.e. physiotherapy-newyork.com. If someone searches on 'Physiotherapy in New York' you are more likely to appear higher up in the results.

Note that it is important to buy your domain name yourself, so that you have ownership of it. Don't be tempted to ask your web designer to do it for you, because if something happens to them you may not be able to access your domain name if you develop a new website in the future.

Purpose built or DIY template website?
There are two types of websites, those that are built from standard templates, or bespoke, personally-designed sites. The latter is more expensive, it can cost hundreds or even thousands of pounds to have a one-off site designed and built, but you do

get (hopefully) a very good site. However, if you have a little time on your hands and a bit of patience, then a template site can easily be achievable for a start-up company. Do bear in mind that your website is the shop window of your business so it must look professional.

A template site is an ideal way to start and can cost very little to set up, the disadvantages are it may not look quite as professional as a purpose-built site and it may take you longer if you're the one who adapting the template! Have a look at Moonfruit as this is a very easy piece of software to get you started. WordPress is better for search engine optimisation (apparently) but does take a bit more concentration! An alternative option is to get someone with a design eye to build a site from an online template for you.

As you would expect, costs for a template site are much lower than for bespoke sites. If you keep your site small, then you can use a package like Moonfruit free of charge which includes free hosting of your site. If you need a little more help, there are companies who provide a choice of templates and who will adapt them for you – get in touch with us if you need advice on this. There is often a monthly maintenance and hosting fee to pay and if you pay extra the company may also help you with search engine optimisation.

If you get a purpose built site then you will usually need to pay for hosting. This should cost around £20 per month or it may come as part of your website builder's package.

It's important to get a quote for a website design and build PLUS get an estimate for how much any amendments will cost once the site is complete. Please note that Google will take positive note of a site that evolves and changes. If a site lays dormant without any changes for months or years, then Google presumes the site is not used that much and will reduce it down the search engine rankings, so your competitors will overtake you! So it is very beneficial to occasionally give your website builder updates, perhaps add an article to your site, new links, or simply change a few sentences to keep the site fresh. This is why it pays to get a quote for amendments up front – better still, get a content management system so you can simply log on yourself to make the changes.

Find out if your website builder will include search engine optimisation (SEO) within the cost.

A photo speaks a thousand words!

Photo library sites are where you can easily and cheaply download images for your website.

As mentioned, do make sure you properly download these after paying for them rather than just copying them as copyright laws apply, and the fines are very heavy!

The images you choose should be relevant to the topic on the page they are loaded to. Remember, if you don't have copyright the fines are massive – don't even risk free images on Google Images as you don't know who loaded them and we know of people who have received fines of £50,000 from photo libraries for using illegal images which were downloaded from Google. You have been warned!!

Calming or therapeutic images can be downloaded for a very small investment and you then have lifelong use of them. Remember to download small or low-resolution images for web use but you need high resolution for leaflets and printing.

Words are key on a website

On the home page, less is more!

You only have a few seconds to capture a reader's attention – if they can't see what they're looking for they'll leave the site in search of something more relevant.

The main message here is to tell the client the advantage of coming to you. This means you need to communicate the benefit to them of your service. So don't just say what you do, for example hypnotherapy – how will that client benefit from the hypnotherapy?

This is where bullet points in a prominent place detailing the services you cover and the benefits are valuable:

1. You can easily link the bullet points through to a separate page detailing the topic for the more analytical reader.
2. They are easy to read.
3. You get your point across concisely.

Looking at competitor sites is a good way of seeing what other people are doing and what works. Obviously you cannot just 'lift' other people's work as copyright laws apply – but this gives you a starting point.

Try to get the passion you have for your therapy across though. If you talk about how you feel and what you like about your therapy it appeals to the clients.

Remember, never promise outcomes or make guarantees. We are bound to keep our copy legal, decent, honest and truthful. In the UK it's worth visiting the Advertising Standards Authority's website http://www.asa.org.uk/ or http://www.cap.org.uk/ to check what you can and cannot say. The Complementary and Natural Healthcare Council have advice you can also refer to and so can your usual regulatory body, but bear in mind that it's the ASA who have the final word.

Call to Action

Ensure there is a way for the client to contact you on each and every page.

This could be a simple 'contact me' button which takes the client to the contact page or you may wish to list your telephone number on each page.

It's best not to put your email address on the website as this will attract spam, have an 'email me' button which has the email address hidden behind it.

Social Media

Promoting yourself online needn't be costly. Whilst we recommend that you set aside some budget for Google AdWords, there are plenty of free ways to make your presence felt. Facebook and Twitter are two of the more popular forms of social media and we recommend that you have a presence on at least one of these.

Although they are free, you still need to invest time and energy into making social media work for you. Set aside some time every week to increase the number of people following you and above all, interact with them – be social. Comment on their posts, share useful information about your therapy or general health and well-being issues and limit the number of 'sales' messages to one in every seven or eight posts. Remember to link back to your website too, as this helps with your search engine rankings.

People either tend to love or hate social media, a bit like Marmite! You do have to bear in mind that these days Google gives much more 'Google Juice' (credence) to your website if you have visitors arriving from social media. So bite the bullet on this one, bear in mind you only have to learn it once, don't let it take over – limit your time on it, but make it work for you.

You are your own marketing machine!!

Most importantly of all, you are the face of your company!

For instance, when you walk into a supermarket, if one of your clients is with a friend and nudges them to say "there's my therapist who's really good. . . " but you walk in looking as though you have the weight of the world on your shoulders, then is that friend likely to approach you? We're not saying that 24/7 you have to go around with a constant smile on your face, but do be more aware that you are conveying an impression of how you would be in a session with your client – even when you are queuing at a supermarket checkout!

You are your best promotional asset!

Deborah (Debs) Pearce and Nicola (Nic) Griffiths are two hypnotherapists who between them have 50 years' marketing experience. As well as running their busy practices, they also head up Therapists Marketing Solutions to help therapists attract more clients. Therapists Marketing Solutions was set up because Nic and Debs saw over 90 per cent of therapists were failing in their first year and wanted to stop this. More information can be found at www.doyouwantmoreclients.com

Chapter Three

Treating anxiety

Anxiety is a very common issue which clients bring to hypnotherapists, so a thorough understanding of what it is and how to treat it is a great building block for any hypnotherapy practice. Fiona Nicolson gives an overview and sets out how you could structure a programme of treatment.

Why do I specialise mostly in anxiety and the impact of trauma on clients? I enjoy the fact that anxiety is just a symptom and that trying to find the root cause of the anxiety leads through a maze of different client beliefs and experiences. All hypnotherapy is detective work, but I think that anxiety requires possibly even more unravelling of feelings and responses.

I enjoy finding and following a 'thread' that might manifest currently in a day-to-day level of anxiety that is stopping a client from going to work or interacting with friends. I find it fascinating to track that thread or threads back to the origin or work with it in other ways to effect a change that will free the client to live their life in the way that they want to.

Clients can exhibit an array of different anxieties, whether it is an underlying day-to-day level of anxiety, panic attacks or symptoms of Post Traumatic Stress Disorder (PTSD). Clients exhibit anxiety as a core expression of their underlying issue; anxiety is the symptom, not the cause. It is also important to recognise that a level of anxiety and stress can be a normal, if difficult, part of life, affecting individuals in different ways and at different times. It is when those levels reach a certain intensity it can start to impact greatly on how an individual lives.

What is anxiety?

The Oxford English Dictionary defines anxiety as: "A feeling of worry, nervousness, or unease about something with an uncertain outcome." An uncertain outcome and a lack of definable cause are the important and common themes of definitions for anxiety and it is also relevant to note that anxiety is intensified in most cases by the inability to define what the cause of the anxiety is and whether the perceived threat is actually real or not.

Anxiety and stress are often confused and the lines between them can be blurred. Stress is something that may come and go in line with specific external circumstance whereas anxiety can persist and the reason for the anxiety is not usually obvious. That being said, anxiety is often triggered when a series of stressful events accumulates and becomes too much for an individual to cope with.

When the level of day-to-day anxiety increases to chronic levels causing significant distress and fear which begins to interfere with work or school and social life there might be a diagnosis of an anxiety disorder. There are six different and definable anxiety disorders, but most clients experience feelings of anxiety without having an anxiety disorder.

Anxiety and modern life

Anxiety is an increasingly common feature of modern life which can affect many of us at different times in our lives and in different ways. Research indicates that the unconscious mind directs an individual's behaviour up to 90 per cent of the time with the remaining 10 per cent being driven by the conscious mind. The unconscious is the older brain system working on instinct and generating habits, based on a response to things rather than a decision-making process. In contrast, the conscious brain is responsible for logical and thought-through processes to try and give meaning to things and a rationale for our behaviour. The conscious experiences itself as being in charge of our behaviour.

A key purpose of our unconscious is to keep us safe and away from what we perceive as potential danger and it uses past experiences to give context to present situations. The unconscious also controls our behaviour during times of strong emotional response.

Even though our caveman days were many, many thousands of years ago, our brains are still evolved for an environment where our survival depends on our unconscious activating a 'fight, flight or freeze' response when we encounter a danger or a hungry predator. It is important to note that the unconscious is unable to differentiate between a perceived threat and a real danger.

When put in a modern-day context, the unconscious is unable to tell the difference between an actual physical threat and the stresses and pressures of modern living and because of this, it can misinterpret things. The unconscious may perceive that a difficult or uncomfortable situation is in fact a danger, tripping the fight or flight or freeze response and evaluating afterwards that such situations should be avoided in future.

Anxiety is in essence how we experience the physical and associated psychological aspects of the fight or flight or freeze response in our modern-day context. Anxiety is an unconscious response in the present to perceived and potential danger in the future. The unconscious uses past experiences to project likely future outcomes, whether the client is aware of these projections or not.

How we respond to perceived danger

The fight, flight or freeze response is a range of physical reactions which prepare the body to either fight a perceived threat, take flight to remove the individual from the perceived threat or in some instances, the individual will 'freeze' in the hope that the predator will not notice them.

This response has been with us since our caveman days and evolved to keep us safe from the hungry predators who might otherwise have threatened our survival. When we become aware of a danger or perceived threat, the fight or flight response is activated and a sequence of nerve cells start firing, with a surge of chemicals like adrenaline and cortisol being released into the bloodstream causing the body to undergo a series of very dramatic changes. This surge of adrenaline, cortisol and other stress hormones accounts for the huge amount of strength that we can suddenly gain in order to protect our loved ones or act heroically to save others.

Heart rate and blood pressure increase, glucose levels in the blood are elevated and blood is diverted away from the digestive tract and directed into muscles and limbs to allow the required extra energy and fuel for running and fighting.

Awareness intensifies, sight sharpens, and perception of pain diminishes as we become ready on both a psychological and physical basis to protect ourselves. We scan our surroundings, looking for threat and once the fight or flight response is activated, there is a tendency to perceive everything in the environment as a threat.

I explain this to clients, who are experiencing day-to-day anxiety, that it's as if their unconscious mind and body are on high alert, scanning constantly for danger – in effect, they are stuck in survival mode.

Clients usually nod at this point, finding a level of relief in the understanding of what and why they are experiencing the many facets of anxiety.

If the response was triggered when faced with a real physical threat, the physical reaction of either running or fighting would ensure that the extra energy and chemicals generated were utilised. In a modern context where the threat is usually perceived and not physically real, the chemicals and fuel are not used up. If our response mechanism is triggered on an ongoing basis, as with day-to-day anxiety, being held in this 'survival' state long term can impact on the immune system and health.

What causes anxiety?

The main causes of anxiety can be the inability to cope with a series of stressful events or the impact of a specific and traumatic event or events. Anxiety can also be a learnt behaviour; clients will often talk about how they remember a parent or sibling being anxious whilst they were growing up.

The likelihood is that these are not mutually exclusive causes, but may all contribute and accumulate, leading to anxiety. I often find that they are not separate scenarios but overlapping factors.

Differences between anxiety and stress

Stress is usually a specific response to a specific external circumstance. Common circumstances that trigger stress are issues with work or relationships or financial problems. Stress is something that can come and go in line with a specific trigger whereas anxiety can persist and the reason for the anxiety is not always obvious.

A client's interpretation of what makes up a stressful situation is subjective and is an accumulation of their learnt beliefs and values both about themselves and their environment, based on past experience.

No two clients will perceive situations as anxious or stressful in the same way; their set of experiences and factors will be unique, hence their interpretation will be unique.

For some people, anxiety is triggered by a recognisable cause such as a trauma, serious illness or a high number of stressful factors occurring either at once or in quick succession. But for many sufferers of anxiety, they are unable to pinpoint the specific and identifiable reason for the anxiety and this can further contribute to their distress.

Clients who are experiencing anxiety can often think that on some level they are going mad and it can help them to understand that anxiety is a normal response to a wide range of triggers and stimuli and has been a part of our physiological make up since the Stone Age.

Recognised types of anxiety

As well as anxiety as an experience or feeling, there are six different and definable anxiety disorders: anxiety disorders are conditions where anxiety is the core symptom. These disorders can overlap, for example someone with General Anxiety Disorder (GAD) or Social Anxiety Disorder can experience panic attacks when they reach a certain level of anxiety or in response to a specific trigger.

Specific Phobias
A phobia is an intense fear when an individual is exposed to a specific object or situation.

Common phobias are flying, dogs, cats and heights. Phobias

can cause individuals to avoid everyday situations. This topic is explored fully in a separate chapter in this book.

Post Traumatic Stress Disorder (PTSD)
This may develop following exposure to any one of a variety of traumatic events such as violent assault, sexual abuse or military combat. PTSD can develop in any situation where a person feels extreme fear, horror or helplessness. The traumatic event could even be witnessed or learnt about rather than directly experienced.

Social Anxiety Disorder
Sometimes called social phobia, this involves self-consciousness about social situations. This can often be based on a fear of being judged by others.

General Anxiety Disorder (GAD)
Is an overwhelming fear, tension and worry, again often without a definable cause or reason. GAD develops in about one in 50 people at some stage in life with twice as many women as men being affected. It often develops first in a person's 20s and can persist long term.

Panic Disorder
Individuals can experience recurring and regular panic attacks. Symptoms can include chest pain and palpitations and it can be common with the initial panic attack that people think that they are having a heart attack.

Obsessive-compulsive disorder (OCD)
This involves certain fears and thoughts that can cause individuals to go through specific routines or rituals. The thoughts are called obsessions and the routines are called

compulsions; common compulsions include hand washing and utilising specific sets of numbers.

Symptoms of anxiety

Because of the fight, flight or freeze response, anxiety involves a wide range of physical symptoms as well as emotional ones. Symptoms tend to vary from client to client, especially the emotional aspects of anxiety and clients often talk about anxiousness, fear or feeling edgy but these sensations and feelings and how a client perceives them are subjective.

Common Physical Symptoms of Anxiety
- A noticeably strong, fast or irregular heartbeat
- Trembling or shaking
- Shortness of breath
- Stomach ache
- Feeling sick
- Dizziness
- Headaches
- Dry mouth
- Excessive sweating
- Difficulty falling or staying asleep
- Muscle aches and tension
- Lack of concentration
- Fatigue
- IBS

Common Emotional Symptoms of Anxiety
- Irrational and excessive fear and worry
- Irrational negative thoughts
- Catastrophising or anticipating the worst
- Sense of dread

- Feeling constantly 'on edge'
- Feeling constantly vigilant and apprehensive
- Irritability
- Mind going blank
- Feeling detached or unreal
- Wanting to avoid specific situations

Working with clients to change anxiety

Initial contact
Clients get in touch with me either because I have been recommended by someone or they have found me through my website and sometimes a parent will contact me because their son or daughter is experiencing anxiety.

The late teens and early 20s is a particularly common age for anxiety to surface, as the person makes the transition towards increased independence, feels the pressure of exams or coursework and moves towards full-time employment or university and further education.

I like to speak to every potential new client on the phone before I agree to work with them, especially in the case of a parent keen for their anxious offspring to work with me. I learnt the hard way initially when a reticent and anxious teenager would be left at my door not knowing what to expect and not really wanting to be there!

Helping clients to begin to understand their anxiety

In the initial phone call with potential new clients I will ask them to explain the current issues that they are experiencing and what it is they would like to change. If there seems to be a wide and complex history, I ask if they could send me an email summarising their childhood, any early issues, life to date and their current key issues. Clients can also benefit from writing down their problems as it allows them to organise their thoughts and develop additional perspectives.

I read this summary prior to the first session and it can be really helpful to have an overview before taking a case history.

I then briefly explain to the client, the role of the unconscious in governing up to 90 per cent of all our behaviour and how the primary role of the unconscious is to keep us safe, secure and away from perceived danger. I talk about how anxiety is the manifestation of the fight and flight response and how their unconscious is actually working really hard to keep them safe and secure. Many clients at this stage say how that makes sense. Within that initial conversation, I highlight that this is a joint therapeutic approach with most therapy taking place between sessions. Many people who experience anxiety feel in some way that they are going mad – the emotional feelings and physical symptoms can be overwhelming, seemingly without cause and any explanation as to how and why they are experiencing anxiety can be reassuring.

Importance of a flexible approach

As a cognitive hypnotherapist, I am trained and qualified to use a variety of techniques and interventions as well as hypnosis. I explain to clients that I dip in and out of different techniques such as Neuro Linguistic Programming (NLP) and Eye Movement Integration (EMI) at different times with different clients because each client's anxiety has a unique set of causes and influences and will therefore benefit from a flexible approach rather than a one size fits all methodology.

We all experience, interact and make sense of the world around us through our five senses. The five senses are sight or Visual, hearing or Auditory, touch or Kinaesthetic, taste or

Gustatory and smell or Olfactory. It is these senses that are known as the representational systems because they are the main ways through which we interpret and give meaning to our experiences. We potentially use our senses all of the time but we each tend to favour one of the senses over the others in how we interact mostly with our world. This is known as our preferred representational system.

Through observation a therapist can gauge a client's preferred representational system which then allows the therapist to communication with the client using language that is familiar and has most meaning to them, that is referring to 'seeing' a problem when working with a Visual client as opposed to talking about 'feeling' a problem when dealing with a Kinaesthetic client.

Initially using representational systems to understand my client's model of the world and how they interact with their world (everyone's perception of their world is different, it is the accumulation and interpretation of their unique experiences and circumstances), this allows me to communicate with clients using their preferred representational system, helping to quickly develop rapport. Good rapport between client and therapist is key to highly successful therapeutic outcomes.

Once rapport is established, I work to understand the client's anxiety, their anxiety pattern (how they 'do' their anxiety) and their solution state (how they want to be without their problem or issue) through specifically-developed questioning which also helps to define the client's core identity and their beliefs and values. Because of a clear definition of the client's solution state it is easy to calibrate and understand results as we move through the therapeutic process and the clients themselves are able to recognise and appreciate the progress that they are making.

Having developed rapport, taken a case history and at this stage understood as far as possible the parameters of the client's anxiety pattern, I would then begin to use a range of interventions and techniques to start reframing the problem and interrupt the problem pattern.

Calibrating anxiety and related feelings and beliefs

I calibrate clearly the client's level of anxiety and related feelings in every session and during interventions (anxiety rarely presents on its own so it's worth identifying what other feelings are present and what else is going on).

I use Subjective Units of Distress Scale (SUDS) which most importantly allows clients, as well as me, to really understand the ways in which their feelings and responses are changing. This makes it easy to define when therapy is completed and when a client has reached their solution state. I also find it helps to use these calibrations when a client sits down at the beginning of a session and tells me that they don't really think they have changed since the last session. When we go through the specific and clear calibration of how they feel now versus previously, there are nearly always changes that they otherwise would not have recognised. This feedback, using their own interpretation of their own feelings, further strengthens their belief in the process and the potential outcome of therapy.

I also use SUDS for a range of questions to define how and what the client perceives they feel and believe about themself. This also helps them to start questioning and understanding their own belief system. I ask questions ranging from "How much do you like yourself?" through to "How capable are you?" and "How much do you enjoy life?" (See full list of questions under Session 1). I will ask clients to 'park the rationalisation' and calibrate their internal feelings and how they feel within themselves, not, for example, the level of confidence that they show the world.

It is interesting to be able to start spotting clusters of answers which are particularly low or high and the inter-relationship between the answers and how they change over a few sessions. Clients who consult me for issues with anxiety often and unsurprisingly score very low on questions such as "How safe or secure are you?", again highlighting the impact of the fight or flight response. Over a few sessions, if most individual or clusters of calibrations are reducing apart from a specific one or two then it can give a strong indication of which belief or feeling should be worked with to further progress towards the client's solution state. There is a self-administered questionnaire available for measuring anxiety known as a GAD-7, which some practitioners send to clients to complete before the first session. There is also another form called a PHQ-9 which measures depression. Both forms are becoming increasing important, both for risk assessment purposes prior to working with clients, as well as gathering information which could be used at some point for research purposes. Both forms can be found online.

Client sessions

I usually spend in region of 90 minutes with the client in Session 1 and up to 70 minutes in subsequent sessions.

Session 1

With most cases of anxiety, I will take a full case history and aim to do some sort of intervention in Session 1 such as time line regression or whatever is appropriate to begin changing the client's problem pattern. I will also take time to work with the client in a trance state, delivering indirect positive suggestions in order to move the client towards their solution state.

Case history
Once a client is settled, I will ask them to again tell me what has

brought them to see me and the current issues they are facing and I will ask them about the current feelings that they are experiencing. Different clients will use different terminology for their anxiety; some may also call it nerves, panic, worry or fear. I always work with a client's own specific terminology.

Questioning techniques
I will get the client to calibrate their anxiety out of 10 (SUDs) and I will ask whether it is a day-to-day feeling, if not I will ask about the frequency of feeling and whether there is a specific pattern during the day, evening or night. If the client suffers from panic attacks, I will want to understand frequency of attacks, the triggers if they are able to pinpoint them and the relationship between the panic attacks and their anxiety. A simplistic response could be, "The anxious feeling starts at about 6/10 and as I think more and more about going out with friends that night the feeling increases and when it gets to 9/10 I have a panic attack."

I will ask when in their life they first noticed the anxiety and what else was going on at that time. I want to know what makes this feeling worse or specifically triggers it (examples could be, being overloaded at work, seeing parents or social situations) and I will want to know what makes it better (this could be things such as being alone or with other people, or downtime at weekends). I will also ask them when else they experience this feeling in their lives, for some clients it could be whilst travelling abroad or when a new boss asks them a difficult question. I ask the client where they feel this feeling in their body. I will say: "If you were to know where in your body you feel this feeling, where would it be?" I ask the client to start thinking about the submodalities (SMDs) of the feeling.

I will ask the client about other frequent and familiar feelings that they experience, whether day-to-day or situation specific. Answers can vary from being lonely to feeling judged or sad or not being good enough and I will go through the same questioning format as above for each feeling.

Working with submodalities
Submodalities are the structural building blocks of representational systems and by manipulating the submodalities of a feeling, (the colour, texture, temperature, weight, location etc.) the feeling can be altered and changed. For some clients, the manipulation of the colour will elicit a shift in the feeling and for others a change might take place when the location or temperature of the feeling is altered.

Each individual will have different key drivers, (key drivers are the unique and individual submodalities which, when changed, will bring about a shift in the feeling). Key drivers will be different for different clients.

Working with trance phenomena
Trance Phenomena (TP) are the different 'trances' that clients exhibit as part of their problem pattern. It has been recognised that these TP act almost as the means by which the symptoms of the problem pattern are produced and maintained. By working with the TP that a client is exhibiting, the problem pattern can be changed.

There are nine major TP and the one that is fundamental to anxiety is Age Progression. Age Progression is the mental projection of ourselves into the future (a form of day dreaming) and an anxious response is generated when those future projections become negative or are centred round catastrophising. Age Progression will not necessarily be the only TP exhibited by the client, but it is the one which is the basis of anxiety and will be present in all cases of anxiety. When questioning a client I will be looking for which TP they are exhibiting and will be specifically aiming my positive suggestions at those TP when using a light hypnotic trance and indirect hypnotic language to move the client's focus towards their solution state.

Defining a client's solution state
I will ask the client to define their solution state (how they want to be without their anxiety). I will say: "How would you like to be without this issue, what would you be doing differently, how would you know you were no longer anxious and what would you believe about yourself that you do not completely believe now?"

Insights into the client's belief system
I will then ask the client a series of questions to define what they perceive they feel and believe about themselves. I again ask clients to mark their feelings out of 10. Core range of questions can include:
- How confident are you (internally)?
- How much do you like yourself?
- How much do you believe in yourself?
- How worthwhile are you?
- How good enough are you?
- How much are you yourself?
- How much in control are you?
- How loveable are you?
- How happy are you?
- How much do you enjoy life?
- How free are you?
- How safe/secure are you?
- How vulnerable are you?

If the client has mentioned that they feel something specific or they would like more of something in their lives, if they say, for example: "I feel lost or guilty or I would like to feel joy (element of their solution state)", but this does not seem to be a central day-to-day feeling, I will then calibrate that feeling and add it to the list above.

In addition, I may also ask the reverse of the question to check the client's response. For example, I may ask 'How much do not like yourself?'. It does not necessarily follow that if a client likes themselves 4/10, then they dislike or do not like themselves 6/10. I say to clients that there is no wrong nor right answers and I tell them that I am not trying to catch them out by asking questions in reverse. Importantly, I again highlight to them this is a great way to start to understand their feelings and beliefs about themselves so they can monitor and calibrate their own progress. Not all clients resonate with all the questions and if they seem puzzled by the question or the terminology or if it does not seem relevant to them then I will not pursue an answer and will move onto the next question. The list is not exhaustive and I tailor the questions to what seems relevant to the client's issue and problem pattern. I do not necessarily ask every client every question.It is interesting to note that some clients initially may not want to admit that that they are confident 2/10 and therefore give, for example, an answer of 6/10.

I watch for indications of inconsistency and the unconscious responses that may indicate that this is happening and I may ask the question again towards the end of the case history once rapport and trust are further developed. Again reassuring that I am not trying to catch them out, just keen to get true figures so they themselves can understand their own progress over sessions.

Causes of anxiety
As previously mentioned, the main causes of anxiety can be the inability to cope with a series of stressful events or the impact of a specific and traumatic event or events.

Anxiety can also be a learnt behaviour. The likelihood is that these are not mutually exclusive, but may all contribute and accumulate leading to anxiety. I often find that they are not separate scenarios but overlapping factors.

Working with anxiety: the series of events
Once I have completed the case history, I will start to work with the anxiety or the belief or beliefs that I consider may be at the root of the anxiety.

Many cases of anxiety precipitate from a series of recent and stressful events (there is usually a historical belief that has risen to the surface due to the series of events and has triggered the anxiety) or the anxiety can be more of a general, usually day-to-day, feeling with no specific or recognisable cause. I spend time initially with the client verbally unravelling the events that precipitated the anxiety, helping them to understand that these events and circumstances are separate contributing factors. Even when the series of events may seem to be separate, it is likely that there are common themes and threads that underpin the client's response to the events.

I may also utilise metaphors within the conversation to help the client recognise alternative ways of interpreting the things they have experienced. Most clients find it helpful to start understanding the different areas contributing to their anxiety separately rather than seeing or feeling them as a pot of 'emotional spaghetti'. Remember that many people, who experience anxiety, feel in some way that they are going mad and any explanation as to how and why they are experiencing anxiety can be reassuring.

Working with anxiety - Influencing and Traumatic Events
Sometimes during the case history, a client will reveal that they have experienced high levels of trauma in the past. Their

emotional state whilst recalling and relating the traumatic experience or experiences will give me a good indication of the extent to which the experience is still impacting on them and I will begin to try and assess how much this is underpinning their anxiety.

The client may not connect the event to the anxiety or have any accessible memory of the event – this is not a problem since my approach begins with the feeling, not the memory. Anxiety can be due to a specific traumatic experience, in the instances of PTSD, and it is interesting to note that recognition is increasing for cases of 'Partial PTSD'. These sub-threshold cases exhibit main symptoms of PTSD, but not necessarily all the symptoms on the extensive PTSD checklist.

I prefer to work firstly to clear the negative emotional response to the traumatic event as this can be a strong factor in the development of anxiety and I work on the basis that even if it is not the pivotal factor, it is likely that it could be a contributing influence. If a client presents with high levels of emotional response when my questioning touches on the trauma, the priority has to be to reduce this emotional response otherwise further progress may be limited. I will explain this to the client to ensure that they understand the possible connection of the traumatic event to their anxiety and the process I will use to work with them to change their response. I use Eye Movement Integration (EMI) to change the response to the memories of the traumatic event. Trauma should be managed by a practitioner experienced in working with and managing trauma and I would recommend that the practitioner be trained in either Eye Movement Integration (EMI) or Eye Movement Desensitisation and Reprocessing (EMDR).

There are other techniques such as the NLP rewind technique which can be used to reduce or eliminate responses to memories of past events. My personal preference is for EMI but I might choose to use rewind with a client for whom EMI is not as effective. Different clients respond in different ways to techniques which is why adopting a flexible and fluid approach is beneficial.

Benefits of EMI when working with trauma
Utilising EMI allows me to work to change the client's current response to the trauma without having them relate or discuss the specific details of the incident or events; this means we can work content free.

A traumatic event can have impacted on a client for many years and clients are usually surprised and relieved that we are able to reduce and eliminate the emotional response to the trauma without analysis or discussion.

The client has to be willing to experience the emotions and feelings connected to the trauma as we work quickly to change them. (It may take a couple or more sessions of EMI to reduce the emotional response to the trauma to a level that allows us to work with the remaining anxiety in other ways or for some clients it can be shifted in one session). I may decide to not completely clear the emotions surrounding the trauma at this stage as those feelings and responses can be useful to lead me to other past experiences or beliefs that are part of the anxiety problem pattern.

I will always calibrate responses as we move through therapy and ensure that at the end of therapy the client has an appropriate level of response to any relevant event. For example, if an event was connected to the death of someone close and sadness is part of the emotional response to the event, it may be appropriate that the client is left with a pre-defined level of sadness that, all factors considered, is right for them.

Working with anxiety: learnt behaviour
If a parent or significant adult has exhibited anxious behaviour, a

child may learn that anxiety is the appropriate response to specific situations and circumstances.

When I am taking a case history, it can often emerge that other family members have anxiety. I work with these cases in the same way as I would with other anxiety clients (once the impact of any trauma has been reduced/shifted or the emotional spaghetti of a series of stressful events has been partially untangled).

Working with anxiety: next steps
Once I have begun, where appropriate, to verbally unravel the pot of emotional spaghetti or started to change the emotional responses and associated beliefs arising from a trauma, I will then start to tackle the actual anxiety.

I may choose to work with the specific feeling of anxiety or I may choose to focus on other feelings or beliefs that I think could be intrinsically supporting or driving the anxiety or that could lead me to the root cause or causes of the anxiety. If a client scores 9/10 for the belief that 'I am not good enough' and 3/10 for a day-to-day level of anxiety, then I may choose to work initially to change the belief and then review how that impacts on the level of day-to-day anxiety. That being said, it is likely that by working with the feelings of anxiety, the unconscious would lead us back to an earlier event or series of events that were central to a client absorbing the belief that they were not good enough.

It is key to highlight that there is not a right or wrong place to start – sometimes you might decide to work directly on the feeling of anxiety and other times the starting point might be a day-to-day belief such as 'I am not good enough'. All these feelings and beliefs interact and inter-relate so whether you start working at one side of the equation or the other will not necessarily detract from the therapeutic outcome.

The unconscious uses past experience to project likely future outcomes

It is good to remind ourselves at this point that anxiety itself is an unconscious response in the present to perceived and potential danger in the future. The unconscious uses past experiences to project likely future outcomes, whether the client is aware of these projections or not.

Because of this, I like to work both on the past experiences that have contributed to the current belief system and feelings of anxiety, as well as the future projection of likely and negative outcomes.

I use a cognitive hypnotherapy version of a time line regression intervention to allow the unconscious to pinpoint past circumstances and events that have contributed to the belief system and I work with the client to reframe and positively change the client's learnings from those events. I may also utilise a variety of different interventions during time line regression, if needed to clear related beliefs, to enable the client to fully absorb and utilise the learnings to begin to change their belief system. Other interventions I may use range from Gestalt chair to parts therapy and I may also utilise EMI if appropriate. Because every client's set of circumstances and responses are different, it would be wrong to set out a prescriptive series of steps and I would always recommend a fluid approach to therapy, working with what comes up.

Working with projections of negative outcomes

As well as working with the past experiences that have contributed to the current belief system and feelings of anxiety, it is equally important to work to change the projections of likely and negative outcomes. I approach this through manipulation of the SMDs and using positive future visualisations.

I may also choose to work with this future negative projection earlier in the process, not to clear it immediately, but to begin to 'destabilise' the anxiety and belief systems. I explain to the client that their beliefs, plus any responses to traumatic events or a series of contributing stressful events (in fact any contributing factors), hold their anxiety in a sort of rigid and fixed problem pattern. With visual clients, I describe it as a version of a Venn Diagram. By beginning to destabilise this rigid pattern, it is possible that the interventions and other work that we do can begin to impact more quickly.

As part of their anxiety pattern, the client will be running a projection of the likely and negative future events and will probably not be conscious of doing this. Depending on what their primary representational system is, the client might be running catastrophic scenarios in the form of a movie or stills or possibly a voice or range of voices telling them how dreadful or disastrous it is going to be. For some clients it could be a voice telling them that they cannot do or achieve something. For others it may be the feeling that things are just going to get worse and worse. I work to change these projections through manipulation of the SMDs, clearly calibrating to understand the client's key drivers.

Positive future outcomes and visualisation
A key part of all of the work I do with clients is utilising positive future outcomes and visualisation; moving the client away from the projected negative outcome that is a key element of their problem pattern, and towards their positive solution state instead.

Within cognitive hypnotherapy we use 'WordWeaving' which in essence is the creation of indirect hypnotic language utilising the client's model of the world and aimed specifically at changing the client's unique problem pattern and the mental processes, such as trance phenomena, within it. After an intervention or at an appropriate point within it, I use a light state of hypnotic trance whilst I use 'WordWeaving' to move the client's focus towards their solution state. There are other techniques that I may use to shift the client's focus towards a positive outcome such anchoring and Swish pattern.

Changing the anxiety through two approaches

In the first session, I will have worked in at least two fundamental ways with the client's anxiety – changing the beliefs that arose from past experiences and moving the focus from projected future negative scenarios towards the client's future solution state.

What can realistically be achieved in the first session?

Again, there is no right nor wrong with this and it really all depends on what you are comfortable with. Some therapists prefer to do the case history in Session 1 and then have the time to mull over the client's story and problem pattern before they start working with the anxiety. Personally, I prefer to utilise the feelings and emotions as they arise and invariably feelings come to the surface during the case history so I prefer to start working with those feelings in Session 1.

If there has been a history of trauma which I want initially to work with, then it is likely that I will take a case history and also work with the trauma in that session. It can also be the case that I will postpone the case history if the client becomes distressed when talking about the trauma and work with the feelings as they come up. I will then revert to taking the case history at a later and appropriate time.

Between sessions

At the end of the first session (and also after subsequent sessions if the client's solution state has changed) I record a download for the client to listen to each night before they go to sleep.

Within the download I deliver positive suggestions based on the client's solution state and how they want to be without their problem, also utilising the trance phenomena that they have exhibited. The suggestions I create for the download give me ample opportunity to ensure that every angle of the client's problem pattern is covered thoroughly.

How long between sessions?

Many therapists like to see clients on a weekly basis, but I prefer to leave it longer between sessions unless I am working with a client with high levels of trauma. I usually leave a minimum of two weeks between Sessions 1 and 2 and then judge progress but prefer to leave three weeks between Sessions 2 and 3. I have found that clients take time to mentally process the work we have done and it is best if they have the opportunity to start seeing the changes in action.

Session 2

At the beginning of Session 2, I will ask the client how they are and what has changed since the initial session. Some therapists, especially at the beginning of their careers, feel more comfortable having made some plans for Session 2 but I have found that clients tend not to respond in the specific ways I might have anticipated and even slightly planned sessions just go out of the window. As previously mentioned, I prefer to go with what comes up, believing that everyone has the resources they need to change and that their unconscious mind will give me an indication of what direction to take by the changes that have or have not taken place.

Once I have an overview from the client as to how they are, I will review the calibrations from Session 1 asking whether they are the same or different. I will also ask them: "How do you know things are different?" in order to understand the specific ways things are changing. If there are feelings or beliefs that are the same where I would have anticipated a change, I will question further, looking for changes in colour or location or frequency of feeling etc. If I had not defined any of the SMDs in previous session for that specific feeling or belief, I will ask the client what the SMDs were previously and then phrase the question 'If it was red before, what colour is it now?' presupposing that a change has taken place.

Once I have calibrated on all or the key elements of the problem pattern, I will then feedback the changes to the client to ensure they realise the extent of their progress and will make comments such as "Great start!" to ensure they begin to recognise that any progress is because of themselves rather than thinking that I have waved a magic wand. I like to work with clients so they initially believe in me, then believe in us (our therapeutic relationship) and then believe in themselves.

If I am working with a traumatic event, I will want to know how the client feels and responds when they now recall the trauma and how any changes have impacted on their anxiety and belief system. I can then decide whether we need to work further with the trauma or aspects of it or whether we can now turn our attention to other parts of their problem pattern.

Changes in problem pattern

Once I have an understanding of the changes that have taken place I can then decide how to progress in Session 2. The intervention that I decide to use in Session 2 and the aspect of the problem pattern that I will target is based on what parts of the problem pattern and belief system have changed and equally what have not. For example, if I had worked with the feeling of 'being lost' in Session 1, which was then 9/10 on a daily basis and it is now down to 5/10 daily, I will check the impact this change has had on the client's anxiety level.

Let's say the anxiety level has dropped from 9/10 daily down to a level of 6/10 but when I calibrate on the general feelings and beliefs I notice that although many of them have positively changed, there is a cluster of some, perhaps: 'I am not good enough'; 'I am not worthwhile'; and 'I do not believe in myself' that have not changed.

My approach in Session 2 would therefore be to work with whichever of the 'no change' cluster of beliefs I think is most important – I may ask the client which feels most significant to them.

Again, there is no prescriptive way I would work, preferring to choose an intervention that is right for the client and the problem pattern at that moment.

As in Session 1, I will take time to work with the client in a trance state, delivering indirect positive suggestions in order to move the client towards their solution state.

Subsequent sessions

I approach subsequent sessions in very much the same way as Session 2.

I define what changes have taken place or areas where there have been no changes and I then decide what part of the problem pattern I will target and what I need to do in order to bring about further shifts. Having completed the intervention, I will then use 'WordWeaving' to bring the client's focus towards their solution state, bearing in mind that their solution state may be different from the previous session.

How many sessions are enough?

Potential clients often ask me this question and I have found that I see anxiety clients slightly more than my client average of three or four sessions. I probably see anxiety clients about four or five times, but this is not set in stone.

When is therapy finished?

Is therapy finished when the client has reached their solution state and their anxiety is 0/10 day to day?

For me the answer is 'no', therapy has finished when the client has arrived at the stage where they are managing their own therapeutic process.

Through the work we have done, the client's unconscious has re-learnt what it needs to do to keep changing and healing and moving towards a changing solution state. Solution states are not static; they alter in line with our new perspectives of both ourselves and our world. Many clients reach a nice, neat conclusive finish to their therapy but equally many others finish therapy just before that ending has been achieved. I used to wonder why clients would cancel an appointment just as they were doing so well. Now I realise that it is because they have reached that place that allows them to continue their own therapeutic process.

Other aspects of therapy

I tell clients that there are two aspects to the therapeutic process, the therapeutic aspect and also what I often call a training or new skill aspect. The training aspect may include the client learning a new and appropriate skill to support themselves, for example, if I am working with a client who has experienced multiple and separate rapes then part of the training aspect of the therapeutic process could be to learn a form of self-defence. The client benefits not from just from being able to physically defend themselves, but more importantly from the knowledge that they have the ability to defend themselves and the feeling of control and confidence that this can potentially give them.

Another part of the 'training aspect' is, where relevant, to help clients understand what element of their problem pattern is a learnt response or behaviour and what part is an intrinsic or 'hard wired' part of their personality.

For example, if I am working with a client whose anxiety is due to social situations and I suspect that they are an introvert, I will talk to them about the 25 per cent of the population who are introverts. I will suggest that they read about being an introvert, how introverts like to be and how they best operate in their world and the differences between introverts and extroverts. It is often as though these insights give a client the recognition that it is OK to be how they are in their world.

They are still working towards changing their anxiety and responses in social situations but now understanding that it is OK not to want to be the life and soul of the party and to need time to recharge their batteries after interacting with others. I am usually wary of giving clients labels for how they respond or feel, but occasionally the insights and understandings that come with a label can be extremely useful for the client.

Tasking between sessions

I am a huge fan of tasking between sessions. It encourages clients to take an active rather than passive role in the therapeutic process and to take responsibility for themselves. It gives the client the message that they can take control of how they feel about themselves and situations and also how they respond to situations and others. Tasking can include aspects of 'training' as above plus using any new techniques that I may have taught them. Tasking should be appropriate to the client.

Case Study

Case studies are published with permission of the client. Names have been changed to ensure confidentiality. Additional case studies of working with anxiety are available on the Hypnotherapy Handbook website.

Case Study

Session 1

Susan is 42 with no prior history of anxiety. Ten months ago she began to experience anxiety when she had a row on the phone with her mother who had refused to take down photos of Susan's ex-husband (Susan had divorced three years previously).

During their marriage, the ex-husband had propositioned Susan's daughter (he was not the girl's father) and Susan had discovered that he had been looking at inappropriate material online. They separated and divorced shortly after. The day after the row with her mother, Susan was in a training meeting at work and experienced a panic attack and was sent home.

Susan's symptoms had become worse over the 10-month period and when she initially contacted me, she had been signed off from work for two weeks. She described her anxiety at 8/10 day-to-day with many of the anxiety symptoms synonymous with the flight or fright response – pounding heart, stomach cramps, perspiring and jelly-like legs.

She felt the feeling she called anxiety in her stomach and it was black in colour. It became worse when there were expectations of her from family and she felt better when in a work situation until demands were put on her at which point the anxiety would shoot up to 10/10 – this happened up to three times per day. She was finding it increasingly difficult to communicate with people as she would stumble over her words and was becoming more and more unsociable.

Susan felt criticised by her mother – she often heard her mother's voice saying: "You are not as good as you think you are". She heard the voice within her head on the left-hand side.

As we went through Susan's case history she told me about the sexual abuse by a school teacher she had experienced at the age of 12 which lasted for up to a year. Susan became very distressed whilst telling me about this.

She had not felt able to tell anyone at the time and felt helpless and powerless. It still impacted on her life and she felt that she was carrying it with her all the time.

I calibrated Susan's feelings and beliefs about herself with the following responses:
- Internal confidence 3/10
- In control 4/10
- Self belief 3/10
- Not good enough 10/10
- Relaxed 2/10
- Free 2/10
- Overwhelmed 9/10
- Safe 2/10
- Strong 2/10
- Brain in overdrive 9/10

Susan's solution state was to be free from the anxiety, relaxed and self-confident, more sociable and able to chat and wanting to move forward because she could believe in herself and that meant that she could be in control.

We discussed the possibility that the anxiety could be linked in some way to her experience of the abuse and by using EMI to change her response to the memories of the abuse we would be able to gauge the impact on her anxiety and work to further clear it using other techniques from that point.

Susan was keen to do this and we spent the reminder of Session 1 using EMI to reduce Susan's emotional response to the memories of the abuse.

We also worked with the SMDs of her mother's voice – Susan chose to move it outside her head and further away with the effect that she was able to turn the volume off so she could not hear her mother being critical.

I sent Susan a download to listen to each night and asked her to practise the 7/11 breathing exercise which I had taught her.

Session 2

I spent time at the beginning of the second session calibrating what had changed since Session 1. Susan was feeling different and better. The abuse felt different – more distant and in the past but when I questioned her further, there were still some aspects that triggered a strong response, but a very different level of response from Session 1. Her day to day anxiety was down to 6/10 and the stomach cramps were down to every few days rather than daily. I taught her a self-help technique called spinning to take control of the feeling and to be able to change it herself.

She still could not hear her mother's voice as the volume was turned down which felt relaxing.

She was still nervous of speaking to people – previously 8/10 and was now 6/10. She realised that she was frightened of looking stupid. Feeling frightened of looking stupid was a day-to-day feeling at work, stomach, black 10/10.

These were the changes Susan had felt and noticed. Very

positive changes and it was interesting to note how the feelings of free, safe and relaxed had changed more significantly than the other beliefs and feelings. This can be very common when reducing the emotional impact of trauma.

- Internal confidence   3/10 now 4/10
- In control   4/10 now 5/10
- Self belief   3/10 now 4/10
- Good enough   1/10 now 3/10
- Relaxed   2/10 now 5/10
- Free   2/10 now 7/10
- Overwhelmed   9/10 now 6/10
- Safe   2/10 now 5/10
- Strong   2/10 now 4/10
- Brain in overdrive   9/10 now 7/10

My conclusion at this stage was that the trauma from the abuse had contributed to her anxiety and Susan still had beliefs about herself and about situations which were continuing to maintain her problem pattern, driving her anxious response.

I chose to work initially again with the abuse using EMI to further weaken its place within the problem pattern, but I wanted to move to working within other aspects of the problem pattern within that session.

I chose to work with the feeling of 'frightened of looking stupid'. This was not because I thought it was a fundamental belief within the problem pattern but because it was a strong day-to-day feeling that had come up since Session 1 and I suspected that by using this feeling, it could lead us to work with the core beliefs such as 'I am not good enough' etc. This goes back to following the thread that weaves through many aspects of a client's problem pattern. I chose to use time line regression where the fear of looking stupid and 'not good enough' was a belief that came up, which we worked to reframe with new learnings. I asked Susan to practise the 'spinning' in between sessions and continue with the 7/11 breathing.

Session 3
Susan had spoken to her mother since our last session without feeling anxious. Susan felt as though she had control back for this first time in years. Anxiety was still at 6/10 but was no longer daily – down to five times per week. It had changed from black to light grey and was still in her stomach. The fear of being stupid was down to 5/10 and she had started to forget about it sometimes when speaking to people at work. She had been out socially with friends since last session and was able to enjoy it.

I calibrated on prior feelings and beliefs, noticing good changes and chose to work with the actual feeling of anxiety in that session as I was interested to understand where that would take us. I again used time line regression back to prior events and we initially reverted back to the abuse with a key emotion of anger which I used EMI to change. We then skipped to a recent relationship where Susan felt rejected and we worked to reframe the rejection and actually then went back to the rejection Susan felt from her relationship with her mother. I chose to use a version of Gestalt chair to work with the rejection.

Session 4
Susan's anxiety was down to 3/10 and she was frightened of it returning. I used the drop through technique to change the fear and anchor the final positive feeling of joy. She now felt that she was moving towards being free of the anxiety and able to believe in herself, which was up to 7/10 and she felt that she had more control in her life; all key elements of her solution state.

I spent more time in this session working with Susan in trance using 'WordWeaving' to keep moving her towards her solution state and the future that she wanted.

We agreed that Susan would get in touch if she needed to after a couple of months once she had had time to fully process all the work we had done and if there were any further things that she would like to tweak.

Conclusion

I hope that this chapter has helped you to have confidence to work with anxiety clients. I would reiterate that there is no right or wrong way to do things or place to start – follow your instinct and your experience as it grows and remember that all feelings and beliefs interact and interrelate so whether you start working at one side of the equation or the other will not necessarily detract from the therapeutic outcome. Go go with what comes up, your client's responses will guide you. I hope you come to enjoy working with this fascinating area as much as I do.

REFERENCES
Cognitive Hypnotherapy *Trevor Silvester Matador 2010*
WordWeaving *Trevor Silvester 2009*
The Structure of Magic *Bandler and Grinder Science and Behaviour Books 1975*
Eye Movement Integration Therapy *Danie Beaulieu Crown Publishing 2014*

Fiona Nicolson retrained as a cognitive hypnotherapist following a long career as a senior executive in the pharmaceutical and healthcare industries. Fiona now runs hypnotherapy clinics in Henley on Thames and Harley Street, London and has a particular interest in working with anxiety and trauma. As well as seeing private clients, Fiona works as a therapist for Anxiety UK, Anxiety UK is the largest

*organisation in the UK specialising in anxiety disorders. Fiona also runs clinics for Jamie Oliver's Fifteen Apprentice Programme, offering therapy to apprentices to help them reach their full potential. Fiona is a member of the Editorial Advisory Board for the NCH and writes for The Hypnotherapy Journal. Fiona has also been featured on BBC Radio.
More information about Fiona can be found at www.fionanicolson.com*

Chapter Four

Smoking cessation

Cathy Simmons is one of the leading practitioners working in the field of addictions. Here she explains how natural and normal reward mechanisms are hijacked by smoking and describes a therapeutic intervention which helps re-educate these mechanisms.

Anyone who knows me will know that I am passionate about helping people find a life beyond their addiction, especially smoking because it is one of the biggest killers in this country.

For that reason, I am hoping that what follows will give you some good insights into how to approach working with smokers and how to get the best and most permanent results with them, so that you will be saving lives too.

Imagine that. Doing what you love and saving lives; it can't get much better than that, can it?

I would like to give you some of the essential background that you need to know in order to work well with smokers along with a practical guide as to how to use this in the most powerful way.

Whilst I realise that each person reading this will have a different training, different techniques and different frameworks, I invite you to take the principles of what I am saying and apply the tools that you already have within the framework.

My story

But first, I would like to tell you a little bit about me. You have probably already guessed that I was a smoker. Yes, I'm afraid 20 or 30 a day and, like many of my clients, I tried everything! I tried hypnotherapy, Alan Carr, more hypnotherapy, more Alan Carr, patches, gum. . .You name it! And most of these had some success for a while, but none of them nailed it for me. I struggled through withdrawals and cravings and in every case, always ending back with the old cigarettes.

However, one day, I walked out of an office in Harley Street and just *knew* I would never have another cigarette again.

My curiosity piqued, I just had to find out what it was that made the difference. Why had this one worked for me when the others hadn't?

I began training in Cognitive Hypnotherapy at The Quest Institute, which was a fantastic grounding and before I knew it I was cutting my working days in investment banking information technology right down, so that I could start to run a practice.

What I was missing

Top of my list, of course, was helping smokers. To my complete dismay, I realised pretty soon that results were hit and miss. I was not getting consistent or permanent results, even though I was doing everything by the book, including tailoring each session specifically for each client, as we had (so rightly) been taught.

So, what was missing? Here began my search for more understanding, for the knowledge that would make the difference; to close the gaps and lead to consistently great and permanent results for all my clients.

Off I went to study more, reading, research, courses, even going back to university in order to really understand as much as

I could about the addicted brain and what we could do to help.

I am now an addiction specialist and love helping people to a fulfilled life beyond addiction and also training therapists to have complete confidence working with smokers.

I know that this quest for more knowledge and understanding will never end. There is always more and more we can learn and neuroscience is discovering new things every day but I am enjoying every step of the journey.

Hypnotherapy is well-known for being effective for smoking cessation, both anecdotally and from the results of a meta-analysis of over 600 studies (Schmitt and Viswesvaran, 1992), which concluded that hypnosis is the most effective way of giving up smoking. So how come I have had the same conversation over and over again with so many qualified and experienced hypnotherapists not feeling completely confident working with smokers, and new therapists feeling demoralised when they find that what they have isn't really cutting it when it comes to helping smokers.

Hypnosis alone is not enough – there – I said it!
It might seem strange to see a sentence like this in a book about hypnotherapy, but I am hoping that this can equip you to go out and help more smokers and, ultimately, save lives!

I will be giving you a bit of background in what is going on in the mind in the formation and maintenance of addiction and you will soon see that just by having a framework which addresses all of the different aspects of your client's addiction, then it really is possible for them to walk away and never crave another cigarette again. Sound good?

Some useful science

Having an understanding of the science means that, firstly you can precisely target the therapy and understand all other factors that will influence success, and secondly you can explain it to your clients – you have no idea how empowering this is for them.

Your clients will see you as an expert, someone who really knows what they are talking about without judging them, building trust and rapport.

Firstly, we need to understand that we are all equipped with natural survival systems; systems that regulate many things that are necessary in life, giving us the desire to eat and drink, followed by the feeling of being sated.

The systems that give us the drive to... ahem... procreate, are the same systems that gives us that niggling feeling at night about whether or not we double locked the front door, until it bothers us so much that we get up to check, followed by the feeling that everything is OK now.

You can see that if we never had any motivation to eat, for example, we would forget and the human race would die out.

The same systems are also involved in our desire to push ourselves further, so that when we first achieve something, it feels amazing, but after a while it just becomes normal, and we want to learn or achieve something more.

Again, such a natural thing, and the systems that keep us motivated to seek out the things we need to live and to learn and grow and do everything else that we need to live well, physically and emotionally.

All drugs, including nicotine, hijack these natural survival systems of the human brain.

How the chemicals work

There are three main chemicals at play in our motivation and reward circuits.

The first one is dopamine, which you have probably heard of. Dopamine has many functions throughout the brain and body, but in this particular circuit, its role is to motivate. In other words it is the 'gotta have' chemical.

Then there is serotonin. In this story, serotonin plays the role of putting on the brakes and stopping the motivation.

So, when we have eaten enough, serotonin is saying: "It's OK, I've got it", which is just as well or we would never stop eating.

Dopamine plays another part in this 'keeping alive' story, in the reward circuits, in that it is an indicator of salience, in other words it signals that you have just had something that is really important for life, or that you have had a better than expected reward, and the signal goes all the way up to that part of our brain which is involved in choice, the pre-frontal cortex.

Finally, when the pre-frontal cortex gets the message that it is really important for life, or a better than expected reward, it sends a message back down to the limbic system (via a substance called glutamate) to say: "remember this", which leads to our brain taking a snapshot of everything around us when we are getting this thing that is 'essential for life'.

So, what does that all mean? It means that the brain is laying down environmental and emotional cues that predict the availability of things that are important to life, so that these cues start off the whole motivation and seeking process.

Let me give you an example. Have you ever gone into a supermarket and noticed that you are getting hungry?

Why is this happening? Well, the supermarket gives you a better than expected reward – i.e. loads of food availability, so dopamine signals this to the pre-frontal cortex, which in turn, sends the "remember this" message back down to the limbic system, and the brain takes a snapshot.

So next time you are in the supermarket, our survival system recognises it and increases motivation via the 'gotta have' chemical, so that we want to go and get it while we can.

Hijacking the mechanism

That's all very well for eating, safety and procreation, but what has that got to do with drugs generally and nicotine in particular?

All drugs hijack this mechanism by artificially stimulating the production of dopamine in the reward system. Much greater levels are produced even more quickly, which is interpreted as meaning 'this is really important for life' or 'this is a much better reward than expected'. In other words it is training the brain to desire and need the drug and at the same time it is laying down environmental and emotional cues, or triggers, which in turn will lead to cravings.

You will hear these from your clients. "I smoke with a drink", "I smoke after a meal", "I smoke in the car" and similar.

It's a very cruel twist. The very same systems that keep us safe and alive are potentially killing the addict or smoker.

Triggers and cues

Of course, the story is more complex than this, but I hope this gives you an understanding of what is going on and why it is not the smoker's fault. It is not due to some sort of moral failing or weak will. It is not as simple as 'you could just stop if you wanted'. Our whole being has learned that cigarettes are essential for life itself.

The main thing I would like you to really get from this is the true power of environmental cues.

Of course there are emotional cues too, and these are laid down in a very similar way, and can be even more powerful and effective in their job of triggering cravings.

Associations are laid down quicker and deeper when they have some emotional colour to them. Again you will hear these from your clients: "I smoke when I'm stressed,", "I smoke when I'm happy,", "I smoke when I'm enjoying myself,".

The final type of trigger that I want to mention here is an

internal one, created as nicotine starts to leave the bloodstream, and if any of you have ever smoked and gone cold turkey you will probably remember how the decision to quit just seemed to make the cravings worse!

The design of our minds and bodies is quite amazing, and we have a sophisticated internal security system that is constantly checking that everything is OK inside the body, including checking for normal levels of substances in the bloodstream.

So, you have decided to quit smoking. Great! After a while the nicotine begins to leave your body, and your internal security system starts to notice that nicotine levels are getting low. Warning bells start to go off, and the 'normal' rules say you must reach for a cigarette, so here comes the dopamine again.

However, you have decided to quit smoking, so the rational, conscious mind is saying "No. I have stopped smoking," but deep down, part of our mind is convinced that this is a life-threatening situation and so increases the severity of the warning; even more dopamine, ramping up the cravings more and more!

The role of memory

How does our mind resolve the inner conflict? As usual, because of our amazing design, there is a part of the brain which is associated with resolving conflict and decision making, a part called the anterior cingulate cortex, acting as the arbitrator.

Which will win? The conscious, rational mind that has decided to quit smoking, or the ever-stronger warning signals?

Our internal arbitrator doesn't know the answer, so it gets the memory involved. Are there any clues from our past experience that will decide which one is right? Now, if the memory comes back with "Remember how great it felt to be part of the crowd?", "Remember how good it feels to stand outside the restaurant and have a good chat with friends", and all the similar past events. You see where I am going? The more the memory reinforces that smoking is a really good thing to do, the more dopamine is released to strengthen the message and the craving gets irresistible. The conscious, rational mind can't resist, and so it gives in and reaches for a cigarette.

I hope you are beginning to realise the importance of these triggers, in summary
- Environmental triggers
- Emotional triggers
- Internal triggers

The tools to reprogramme the mind
I'm sure that you are already understanding what this means for our therapy. Imagine how powerful it would be to the smoker if you could break all of these associations?

If you could work with them to re-programme the mind to remove those environmental triggers and emotional associations. . .if you could interrupt the process of a craving, so that, when the nicotine starts to leave the system it doesn't lead to picking up a cigarette. And the good news is that you already have the tools to do that.

Hypnotherapy combined with behavioural techniques and the correct information given to the client can do exactly that.

The very first step of the "7 Steps to Smoke-Free Clients" that I teach to hypnotherapists, is 'Know your science' and I hope that you are beginning to understand why.

Imagine your client leaving your therapy room with no more desire for a cigarette, and future proofed against the cues that used to mean them smoking, and this really is possible.

A treatment overview

Every therapist works in their own unique way, of course, so what

I am proposing below, in terms of pre-session, session and post-session structure is just the way that I find works particularly well for my clients. It is typical of my approach, however, all our clients are individuals and there may be circumstances where I would take a completely different approach!

I hope you will find it helpful.

1 The first phone call

Your therapy begins from the minute you are first in contact with your client, whether you are answering their email or picking up the phone.

As a brief aside, my opinion is that if your first contact is by email, I would always arrange a phone consultation before booking them in to see you, for reasons that will become clear.

That first conversation might be difficult for your potential client. There is likely to be a part of them that wants to hang on to the smoking. Remember, deep down the mind 'believes' it is essential for life. The unconscious mind is crying out to smoke, and so the rational, conscious mind needs to make some sense of this and so you will hear "it is a crutch", "it helps me concentrate", "it is my only pleasure", "it's my friend" and so on. Be gentle. It is not their fault!

Somehow, just by letting your potential client know how nicotine hijacks their survival systems is very empowering for them and, in and of itself, can begin to break down any resistance.

Use the time on the phone to build rapport and to reassure them, asking them some of your history-take questions and get them to articulate their solution state. It is all fantastic information for later and you are already beginning to future pace them to their possible life free of the smoking.

If there is only one thing that the client gets from our call, I want them to really 'get' that the smoking is not their fault. This understanding can be a real "Aha" moment for them. They have spent so much of their life beating themselves up for having no willpower, as have their friends and families, quite possibly. Let them know that it is not their fault, and let them know that there is hope, that it really is possible to get free.

This initial conversation is also the time to assess for any contraindications. Be aware of any excessive stress, depression, low mood or evidence of other drug use. All of these factors would influence whether it is in the best interest of your client to come to you to stop smoking, and of course you would take into consideration any other medical factors that would mean that it wouldn't be appropriate to work with that client, e.g. psychosis, or conditions that are not within our field of competence. In my two-day training, I cover some of the circumstances in which it wouldn't be in the client's best interests for them to stop smoking right now, and how best to handle them.

2 Pre-session tasks

Once your client has booked a session with you, they can engage in the process right away. Think about some tasks you can set them, that might start to interrupt their smoking patterns or might start to bring their smoking from being unconscious to conscious. You could think of them as 'mindful smoking' exercises.

I remember asking a client to start to smoke 'mindfully' for the few days before she came to see me. She was to be aware of each cigarette, how she was holding it, the smell, and the sensation of the smoke in the throat, how it looked in her hands etc. Between our first phone call and her coming to see me, I tasked her with only smoking whilst she was doing nothing else and that meant she couldn't smoke while watching TV, having a conversation, reading or any other activities.

She came into my office that day and told me that a very

strange thing had happened. As she smoked 'mindfully', her legs became really heavy and solid. She had felt that every drag was filling her legs with smoke and tar and she really didn't like it at all. The power of the imagination!

Another thing you can do is to ask clients to smoke with the other hand. I know a lady who completely stopped after she broke her right (smoking) arm and it was in plaster.

No matter how hard she tried, she couldn't smoke with her left hand!

Asking the client to change their brand of cigarette for the last couple of days can also move the smoking from unconscious to conscious awareness, which is what we are aiming to achieve.

Be creative (and not too cruel!).

Another thing I would do prior to a session is to send the client a questionnaire to fill in and email back to me in advance.

Having understood the power of environmental and emotional triggers you need to know exactly what these are for your client. What are their high risk times, places, people and emotions?

Have them write down their reasons for stopping, their 'away froms', such as "I hate the smell", "I am scared for my health", "I can't exercise any more", and also their 'towards' reasons for stopping, such as "I want to see my children grow up", "I want more energy", "I want to be free!".

You can use all of this information in the session.

They may have already given you all the information you need over the phone, but many clients find it quite an insightful exercise as they start to think about it much more objectively than they have before in their own time, and quite often they remember important things that they may not have told you. Along with the tasks they are doing, this exercise begins to prime their mind for the change that is to come. It is part of the therapy, which is one reason I like to do this before they come into my office.

The session
Now we come to the session itself. I am, of course, assuming that all possible contraindications have been assessed and that you feel you are clear to work with your client for the smoking. To re-iterate, if someone is very low mood, or clinically depressed, then it is not a good idea to go ahead. Also if the client is in a situation of very high general stress, then it is very likely that one addiction could be swapped for another. Deal with the stress or teach them stress reduction tools before you see them for the smoking.

For most clients, I find that a single session is normally enough. This could be as long as two and a half to three hours, to give you time to cover everything you need. I teach this approach on my training for therapists and this is often met with some surprise. However, once they have tried it with their clients, most are very happy with it and find it gets great results.

Give both of you a little break after about an hour and a half, if you can, because after that time we tend to lose concentration, but you will be surprised at just how quickly the time goes.

The session itself could be quite straightforward. To my mind most of the transformation happens before the 'hypnosis'.

I would just like to add a point about working with other drugs here. All drugs need to be looked at differently, here I am just talking about smoking, and it is generally safe for someone to stop smoking suddenly (apart from the contraindicated conditions), whereas with other drugs, such as alcohol, prescription drugs, skunk and others, it is appropriate to work within a program of managed withdrawal because of the potential dangers of sudden cessation.

Some essential principles and steps to apply in the session itself
1) Prepare
You might think this is stating the obvious, but I am not just talking about having everything ready for the session, your

session plan and any materials for your client. I am talking about preparing yourself.

Unconditional positive regard is essential for us as therapists when working with our clients, and often we have our own 'stuff', especially around smokers.

If you have never smoked it is quite possible that you may have underlying attitudes and beliefs about smoking and smokers that you are not aware of. These might well get in the way of working effectively with clients. Those of us who have smoked may easily fall into the trap of thinking we understand exactly what the client is going through. Remember, everyone is unique. The client's thoughts, triggers and reasons for smoking will be different from ours.

So, give yourself some time to prepare yourself mentally and emotionally before the client comes in.

2) Inform

It is important to inform your client as much as possible. If you explain that the smoking is hijacking their natural survival mechanisms, then they begin to realise that it is not their fault, and this normally comes as quite a revelation and helps to lower any remaining resistance. If you believe there is still some resistance, then you might consider some form of parts work or unconscious ideo-motor signalling to establish and deal with the remaining positive intention of the smoking.

Now, remember what I said about the first few days after stopping? How our internal arbitrator (the Anterior Cingulate Cortex or ACC) tries to deal with the conflicting messages with the low nicotine warnings on one side, and the rational part who has decided to stop smoking on the other. At this point the ACC contacts the hippocampus to see if there is anything in memory which could help with the decision, shall I, shan't I?

Normally, all the supposed positives about smoking are what

come back from the memory, with additional dopamine to make it even more urgent to smoke. But just imagine what would happen if all the real facts come back from memory instead. How there are 4,000 chemicals in cigarettes, 600 of which are poisonous and at least 42 are considered to be carcinogenic. I strongly recommend doing some research so that you have all the facts to hand. What if the memory would remind your client of all their reasons for stopping, the smell, the threat to their health, the slavery. . .?

The amazing thing here is that just by having these facts clear in the memory, then the message does not get any more urgent. No more dopamine is added to the message and the craving actually subsides before it gets too strong. That's right, it becomes just a niggling little feeling which just disappears after a swig of water, a deep breath and a count to ten.

For that reason, I would spend some time going over the facts with them. Once the client realises that it isn't their fault, then somehow they become much more open to hearing the truth about smoking, because it is no longer a part of their identity. It almost becomes a case of you and your client against 'the' smoking. Obviously this does need to be done with sensitivity. If your client is already ill because of the smoking, then they don't need reminding of all the poisons.

If this is the case then I would just remind them of all their own reasons for wanting to stop. Have them write all of these down and carry around with them. Better still, have them make a video of themselves on their phone as they describe all their reasons for stopping. That way, if they have any doubts at any point, all they need to do is watch their video and the great thing is that they will always have it with them.

3) Break the associations: some techniques
I would then take them through a series of techniques or

visualisations to help them break all of those emotional and environmental triggers that they have told you about.

Techniques such as the Swish Pattern (an NLP technique) can be brilliant for this, alongside another technique sometimes referred to as Thought Stopping, which is particularly good for clients who have a lot of internal dialogue.

Thought Stopping
1 Have the client close their eyes and imagine being in a situation where they would normally have a cigarette (for example at the pub with a drink).
2 Ask them to verbalise the inner conversation that leads to them having a cigarette. This could be something along the lines of "All my friends are going for a cigarette. That would be nice, I think I'll have one. . .", or similar.
3 Establish a statement they would rather hear instead and call it a Coping Statement. This could be something like "I know I can do this", or "I am free and healthy". It doesn't really matter what as long as it is your clients own words and it is stated in the positive; in other words, not containing 'Nots' or 'Won'ts' or similar negative words.
4 Ask the client to close their eyes again, imagine themselves back in the situation and ask them to verbalise the inner conversation again.
5 As soon as they say something positive about the situation, then clap your hands and say "Stop!" loudly. Then immediately say their Coping Statement. Of course they normally jump, but by having the unexpected interruption, they have immediately gone into trance and the next statement they hear goes right in at an unconscious level.
6 Do this three times and then ask them to do it silently for themselves another three times.

I find this technique amazingly effective and not just for

smokers. I use it for all sorts of behavioural change, but please be aware that it is not so suitable for banishing negative thoughts or worry and anxiety and I would use something slightly different in those cases.

Use whatever techniques you know to break every one of the environmental and emotional triggers, and your client may never have a craving again.

Of course, you will be reinforcing this later within your suggestions by guiding the client to mentally rehearse going through each one of these high risk times, but as a non-smoker (or whatever they want to call themselves).

Teach Self-hypnosis

I always teach my clients some form of self-hypnosis during the session and this serves two purposes.

Firstly, it is a useful tool for the client for stress relief and mental rehearsal and secondly, it acts as a fractionation exercise, having the client go into trance and getting used to your voice before the official 'hypnosis' bit that they will be expecting. It is also a brilliant excuse to start the mental rehearsal of their happy, healthy life, free of the smoking.

Give your client tools

I am a great believer in empowering our clients.

This is not about having something 'done to' them, it works best as a collaboration and giving them craving and stress-control techniques that they can use for themselves if they feel they need to.

Tools and techniques such as EFT, NLP submodality interventions, 7:11 breathing and the drop-through technique are all great examples.

If any of these are new to you, there is plenty of information available if you search the Internet. Of course, while you are teaching them these techniques, you are also using them to help, either to remove a craving if they have one in the room, or to break the effect of a trigger, for example.

The hypnosis section

The great thing about this approach is that the apparently conversational first half of the session has probably made the most difference. The transformation has already begun.

The final induction and suggestions are, of course, what your client is probably expecting and it is also the time to add two really important elements, specifically a decision point and future pacing.

I am not going to provide a script here, as I genuinely believe that we need to be tailoring our suggestions completely for each client, but I do strongly suggest having both of these elements present.

A decision point
This is a point, during this final trance, when you ask your client to make a final decision, and this can be done metaphorically.

For example, a 'forked road' visualisation where they imagine that they are standing at a fork in the road and there are two possible futures ahead of them. One of these paths, on the left hand side, is their future as a smoker, and you can label that the 'Path of Death' or the 'Path of Slavery'. Be sensitive here, and use your clients' own words.

The other path (the right path) could be called the 'Path of Life', or the 'Path of Freedom', again, use your clients' own words and labels for this.

Have them imagine going down each path in turn and having a good look at each one.

Remind them of their reasons for stopping. Remind them of

everything they told you they hate about smoking as you look down the path of death, and as they look down the path of life, remind them of everything great about their life as a non-smoker; all the things they have already told you in their history take. This visualisation can be very powerful, so please don't rush them. Give them all the time they need to see their own futures in their own way.

When you are sure they really 'get' the difference, then ask them to choose one path, the right path, once and for all, and ask them to tell you which one they choose.

Future pacing
End the session with some powerful future pacing, where the client can rehearse all of their high-risk times, with them as a happy, healthy non-smoker (or their solution words).

Follow up sessions

Whilst I am aiming for a single session to be enough for a client, there will be times when they need to come back, and that is when we, as therapists, might be tempted to feel that this is some sort of failure, either by us as the therapist, or on the part of the client.

All I can say is "Get over it!". This is not about failure, it is about getting more information that we can use to ensure that the transformation is permanent.

So, why might someone come back? Here are some possibilities

1) General levels of stress are high
When stress levels are high, it makes us more sensitive to those messages flying about in our survival systems. This is when it is likely for a client to move from one drug to another, and this will

continue until either the stressors have gone, or until they find some practical way of being able to manage their stress.

It is a bit ironic, because smoking itself raises the adrenalin levels and therefore your client is always in a state of higher stress than someone who doesn't smoke. However, we do need to help them with this first, so it needs careful assessment before deciding if it is the right time for them to stop or not.

2) Specific events
Occasionally life throws us unexpected challenges, a break up from a partner, the loss of a job and so on. If the client reaches for a cigarette during one of these, then it is likely that there is still an unconscious association between cigarettes and the relief of stress.

Help them by assessing the level of general stress and dealing with that, and then go back and break any emotional (and environmental) associations that are still there or have reformed since starting smoking again.

3) Unresolved emotional connections
Quite often there are connections that we missed in the first session. This might happen if the client was not consciously aware of the connection and, if it is strong enough, can motivate them to smoke again.

4) Unresolved environmental triggers
I had a client who stopped smoking easily and happily in a single session; no cravings, no issues. Then, after about six months, I had a call from him to say he had started smoking again. No, there were no emotional or stressful events that had happened. Just the opposite! He had gone on holiday to Spain. The minute he got off the plane in the sun, he had the urge to smoke! Don't underestimate the power of environmental triggers, even after

a fair amount of time has passed. He came back and we dealt with that, and them I taught him future rehearsal techniques to help him break his own associations if he felt there was any event coming up in the future which might present a challenge. I must say that I learned from that experience and now I teach these to all my clients.

5) *Self-destruct*
Sometimes there is a much bigger underlying issue, which we don't always uncover in the initial questioning. Sure, we know that, as far as the unconscious mind is concerned, the smoking has a positive intention for your client, and we work to understand this in the history take or using parts work in the first session. However, sometimes it slips through the net.

So be aware of possible "I don't deserve to be happy and healthy" or "I'm not good enough" beliefs and work with them first.

6) *Having a cigarette*
Having a cigarette will start the whole process going again and can lead to them starting again in earnest, and there could be a number of reasons for this happening other than those I have already mentioned.

One reason might be that they weren't really engaging in your session when they came into your office. I have come across this a few times, when the client really didn't want to stop. It is a good idea to assess the level of motivation, using the SUDS scale, when you first speak to a client on the phone, and see if there is anything you can do in conversation to help them raise their motivation to a higher level. I believe we can still help these clients if we are aware of it.

Too often it is unhelpful or jealous friends that are the reason, and in this case, rehearse with your client what they will say the next time someone offers them a cigarette, and reinforce this in the future pacing in trance. It is always worth pointing out that "hypnosis makes it easy to stop; it doesn't make it impossible to smoke!"

Conclusion

I realise that there is far more that I could share with you than it is possible to include in this chapter, and so I have tried to put across some of the most essential background and some principles around working with smokers and I hope you are realising that, by understanding the science behind addiction, it means that you can target your therapy even more effectively for lasting change.

Above all, I hope you are inspired to go out there and help people get free of the smoking permanently and completely, saving your clients a lot of money and, possibly their lives!

Cathy has a background in Investment Banking and IT in the City where the challenges that go along with the work environment and lifestyle can mean that drug and alcohol use is only too common. Pressures are high and so is availability!

After training at The Quest Institute and qualifying in 2007 with the HPD, DipCHyp and NLP Master Prac., she continued her research and studies into the nature of addiction through countless trainings, including a post-graduate Certificate in Psychology, where she was first introduced to Psychobiology.

Creator of The Simmons Method: a science-based approach to addiction. She runs The Simmons Clinic in London offering gentle help to professionals for a life beyond drug use and addiction; working with smoking, alcohol, cocaine, cannabis and other drugs. She also offers training for hypnotherapists through her Get Complete Confidence Working with Smokers programme.

Cathy is also an NCH Accredited Hypnotherapy Supervisor and Specialist Advisor on Addictions to the National Council for Hypnotherapy. She has the following qualifications: BSc(Econ) Hons, DipCHyp, HPD, MNCH, NLP (MPrac), AccHypSup. Post-Grad Cert: Psych.

If you are interested in sponsoring a training in your area or training school then please contact her on cathy@cathysimmons.co.uk

Please also enquire about training for non-hypnotherapists and additional modules for alcohol, marijuana and other drugs.

Website: http://www.cathysimmons.co.uk
Email: cathy@cathysimmons.co.uk
Email: training@cathysimmons.co.uk
Telephone: 0207 419 7915
Facebook: https://www.facebook.com/SimmonsClinic
Twitter: @cathy_simmons

Chapter Five

Weight loss and management

Steve Miller has a straight-talking, no-nonsense approach. He explains how the blend of hypnotherapy, motivational coaching and an 80-20 eating plan works for his clients.

Over the last ten years I have focused my practice on the niche area of weight management. With obesity levels spiralling out of control, it is no wonder that my practice remains busy and the waiting list grows month on month. With millions already spent on health education and increased awareness of the foods we should eat growing by the day my conclusions are confirmed more than ever. We are a nation addicted to junk food and to suggest food is a drug is, in my opinion, accurate. Weight management is a mind set and as hypnotherapists, we have one of the most valuable tools to help those struggling.

How my experience helps me help

I understand what it is like to be fat. Yes, I use the word fat because it is my belief that wrapping it all up in cotton wool does nothing to reduce the waistlines of obese Britain. I recall the days where I myself sat on the sofa preferring to order in the take away and wash it down with a bottle of wine. Whilst I appreciate many struggle with emotional eating, that was far from the reality of my life. I was fat because I was lazy and had lost my mojo. Eventually I managed to get my head in the right place and after yelling at myself to get my backside off the sofa I managed to lose four stone, which is a lot of weight for someone at five feet seven inches tall.

Over the years I have treated hundreds of fat clients and my success has been acknowledged year-on-year by the media including a hit TV show and features and comments in numerous magazines and national newspapers. I love my work and observing the journey of a client who goes from a staggering BMI to a healthy one is rewarding. But as well as that, witnessing a surge in a client's self confidence makes me realise why I decided to become a niche expert in weight loss and weight management. Hypnotherapy is the primary tool I use in treating my clients, but in addition I utilise a straight-talking motivational coaching style and an eating plan that uses an 80-20 approach in which clients eat healthily 80% of the time and have a bit of what they fancy for the remaining 20%.

At the core of a client's need is motivation, so my energy and passion to help them achieve their goal needs to be visible. They need to feel that I believe in them, and equally experience my energy and determination to drive them to the end result. Given clinical hypnotherapy is associated with the power of suggestion it also means I maintain an ideal weight myself. It will come as no surprise that I do not see how a fat hypnotherapist can support and treat a fat client. It would be similar to a smoker attending an appointment only to find the hypnotherapist smoking themselves.

Our goal is to inspire and to act as a role model all the way through the therapeutic process. If we cannot adhere to that then we should not touch clients presenting with a need to manage their weight.

There have been a number of developments in the hypnotic weight loss arena over the last ten years including the Virtual

Gastric Band. Whilst I appreciate this has its place, we must always remember that many clients will see it as a quick fix and a magic wand, with some failing to apply any effort themselves. Personally I prefer a much more authoritarian model which I have developed over the last twelve months. The authoritarian model forbids clients to make excuses, demands weight loss week after week, and uses a direct and forthright hypnotic style of suggestion in trance. Of course it is what works best for a client, but ten years' experience has taught me that the authoritarian protocol delivers the best results short and long term.

How hypnotherapy helps

We are gifted to have the skill of hypnotising clients in a clinical setting to lose weight. Hypnosis and hypnotherapy will support a client to lose weight in three key areas which I label A,B,C:

Attitude
To be motivated, determined and driven to lose the unwanted weight.

Behaviours
Helping the client to adopt the habits of a healthy individual in control of their weight.

Capability
Supporting a client to understand how to manage emotional eating, boost confidence and live life long term, managing their weight effectively.

I will explore each area to illustrate how a clinical hypnotherapist supports each area.

Attitude

The majority of clients visiting a clinical hypnotherapist for weight loss/management will initially carry a negative attitude about themselves, their ability to lose weight and their future. Hypnotherapists can offer enormous support to a client needing to value themselves better and start believing that they can turn around a life of fat for a life of slim.

Again it is essential the hypnotherapist models an attitude of positivity and demonstrates through their behaviour that they absolutely have belief that the client will achieve a result. For me this out of formal trance experience is what I label 'wakened hypnosis'.

The power of suggestion from the hypnotherapist is not always done in a formal trance when treating weight loss clients. In fact much of the work in driving a positive attitude is done outside formal hypnosis. An example here is where the hypnotherapist encourages the client to take personal responsibility for their lifestyle and weight management. A good hypnotherapist will help the client reframe their thinking and bust any excuses that stand in the way of a successful weight loss. Yes, sometimes the process is challenging and a competent hypnotherapist will always challenge the client where needed to get them to take ownership.

That said, formal hypnosis allows us the opportunity to make a marked difference in the clients presenting attitude. Using a range of hypnotic protocols such as parts dissociation and reintegration, direct suggestion and pseudo-orientation in time, the hypnotherapist can drive the client's optimism, increase their self esteem, and develop their attitude to improve for the better. With a positive attitude in place hypnotherapy can then move to stage two and develop the habits of the client and support the client to behave in a way that supports them in managing their weight long term.

Behaviours

Once the client's attitude is fired up to lose weight and manage it for the long haul a good hypnotherapist will work with the client to help them let go of unhealthy eating habits and install habits that will help the client regain control over food. The absolute goal here is to help the client take back the control over food and help them to increase their motivation to exercise more where possible.

In addition, the hypnosis can be used extremely effectively to help a client who is struggling with emotional eating. When we are stressed we release higher levels of the stress hormone cortisol and whilst cortisol has many benefits, too much of it can cause problems including the triggering of a craving for salty and sweet foods.

Also, when we eat food we experience a natural increase in serotonin making us feel comforted and happier. It is therefore essential a client regains control over the emotion so that they do not eat too much. Hypnotherapy will help programme a client's mind to break the cycle of emotional eating and behave in a more constructive way when they feel stressed.

Different strategies

There are several hypnotherapeutic strategies that can be used to achieve this goal including:

Analytical hypnotherapy

Whilst not my personal preference a hypnotherapist may use the trance state to help the client analyse and understand why their weight is as it is. In a relaxed state the client will be encouraged to allow their unconscious mind to identify the underlying cause for being too fat. The hypnotherapist will then work with the client in hypnosis to let go of the cause and replace the old with something more constructive. For those clients who may be carrying too much weight due to childhood experiences this hypnosis technique can work well.

Motivational hypnotherapy
I am a huge advocate of motivational hypnotherapy. Here the hypnotherapist will conduct a session of hypnosis with a positive, upbeat and energetic style to help the client take control of food and increase their level of excitement to manage their weight effectively. Motivational hypnotherapy is very effective for those clients who feel they have lost their way by falling into bad habits and need to develop a mindset that is determined, focused and excited about being their ideal weight.

Solution-focused hypnotherapy
Again a definite preference of mine is solution-focused hypnotherapy. Here the hypnotherapist will consistently work with the client to identify solutions to any challenges. Wallowing in self pity is not an option as the hypnotherapist encourages and nudges the client to move forward and identify solutions. In hypnosis the client may explore solutions to challenges and once the best solution is found embed it into the unconscious mind.

Capabilities
A professional clinical hypnotherapist will have one special gift to share with their clients which is to be able to teach their clients how to use self hypnosis. This is an incredible and powerful tool and can be used by a client to help them:

- Remain self motivated, determined and excited about managing their weight effectively.
- Embedding the control a client has over food so that they are able to eat less and eat better.
- Boost self belief so at times when stress comes into life it

doesn't mean a client turns to food for comfort. Supporting a client's capability to manage their weight also involves the hypnotherapist offering a range of additional tools. For example I offer all my clients my 80-20 meal plans, a list of foods that are scientifically-proven appetite suppressants, and a number of strategies to help manage emotional eating, such as stress buster and anxiety management techniques.

Importance of exercise

The hypnotherapist who specialises in weight management will also be able to assist a client select appropriate exercise plans, although a client is also encouraged to seek advice from their GP. Making exercise a pleasure rather than a chore is of critical importance and a good hypnotherapist will work with their client to achieve this goal. We have to remember that exercise will bring a huge amount of benefit including a reduction in cholesterol, an increase in mental focus and a boost to a client's self confidence.

And finally building long-term capability is very much about maintaining long-term motivation. Motivation is what drives weight loss and is indeed the powerhouse. Without it a client's weight loss and long-term weight management is doomed. Let's face it, the majority of people start their weight loss journey with motivation brimming over the top, only to find after a few weeks that it has all dried up.

That's why a talented hypnotherapist will offer a number of practical tools that help ensure the client's capability to maintain motivation is strong.

There are two types of motivation I recommend all hypnotherapists use. First you have the 'pull' style motivation which is in other words the things a client is pulled towards; such as seeing themselves fit into a new outfit or being able to play with the kids.

The other style of motivation I recommend is what is known as 'push' style motivation. This is when the client is motivated by the negative consequences of being too fat such as having poor health, or getting so fat a client feels unattractive. The competent hypnotherapist will often use both styles within their treatment plan, ensuring the client remains motivated to achieve the goal.

Hypnotherapy is often referred to as the modern day fix for those looking to lose weight and mange it. More and more people are waking up to the fact that straight-jacket diets just do not work and that weight management starts in the mind. Whilst formal trance hypnosis alone is definitely not the answer to sustainable weight control, combine it with the practical tools needed, and it is now very much a central component to help those needing to eat less, eat better and move more.

The Weight Loss Programme – what to expect

It probably isn't at all as you expect. Most people visiting a clinical hypnotherapist expect a treatment room of Buddha's, soothing music and crystals dangling from the ceiling.

Times have changed and whilst there may be some spiritual elements to the work of modern day hypnotherapists it isn't as explicit as it used to be.

You'll be hard pushed to find any such markings of spirituality in my consulting room, so let me explain. The vast majority of clients looking for support for weight loss do not have a high engagement with spirituality so having a neutral setting in the consulting room is important.

My six week weight loss programme brings a tone of straight talking. If you are looking for tea and tissues throughout then you are in the wrong place.

Of course we spend some time assessing the underlying issues for the weight gain, but a line is soon drawn so that we can move on and get the result the client wants. Sitting wallowing in negative discussion does nothing to reduce the weight and if anything will retain the status quo and even give a client permission to get fatter.

Clients also receive a number of extra tools as we begin the programme including access to a download audio to listen to between sessions, a copy of my latest book *Steve Miller's Slimming Secrets* and six weeks of meal plans using my 80-20 approach to eating.

Here I outline the six session programme so that you can understand how the straight talking hypnotic authoritarian approach works.

The six session programme

Session 1
During session one I conduct what is known as a full case history. I will have checked via email that this style of hypnotherapy is suitable for the client so that we can crack on as soon as the client arrives to the consulting room. We explore fully the underlying reasons for the weight gain and the reasons for wanting to lose weight as these will be incorporated in the hypnotherapy. In session one I also outline the ground rules explaining that the following will apply throughout:

1. Excuses are banned and that if the client faces a challenge during the process they will work to find a solution.
2. I as the hypnotherapist and coach reserve the rights at all time to take the client off my programme if I feel they are not co-operating with the process. The client is informed they will then receive pro rata money back.
3. There will be no blame during the programme and that full

responsibility will be taken to complete tasks as instructed.
4. The client texts me daily updating me on their progress and achievement.
5. If the client does not lose weight weekly then they will be removed from the programme.
Session one always lasts longer than the standard one hour as there is much to cover including meal planning, motivation techniques and the 'keeping in touch' plan between sessions agreement.

Session 2
In session two I teach the client how to use self hypnosis. This involves the client experiencing a session of hypnotherapy and then practising the technique so that when they leave my consulting room they are in a position to use this as a tool to embed new habits. It is vital clients do self hypnosis each day between sessions so that they continue to let go of old habits and begin to embed new ones that are conducive to a healthy and sustained weight loss. In summary, self hypnosis incorporates the following steps:

i) Finding somewhere comfortable, warm and safe to conduct the process.
ii) Closing the eyes to cut out 80 per cent of external distraction.
iii) Gaining a focused concentration by taking the mind into a favourite place.
iv) Counting down from 10 to one so that the trance state is progressively deepened.
v) Dissociating negative habits that have in the past been responsible for a state of being too overweight.
vi) Installing new habits into the unconscious mind that will help regain control over eating habits and increase the level of self motivation to lose the unwanted weight.

vii) Playing the movie of the end result seeing, hearing and feeling the new life as a slimmer person.

viii) Formal awakening from the trance state by counting up from one to ten.

In addition a client will be given a motivational programme using techniques that are appropriate to the client's needs.

Session 3 to 5

During session 3 to 5 the hypnotherapy sessions are tailored to the specific client.

Here I develop a script appropriate to the individual client so that it is makes sense and the client's unconscious mind accepts the suggestions within it.

The formal hypnosis session will last around thirty minutes and for the remaining thirty I agree with the client the actions to be undertaken between the sessions. The hypnosis session is motivational and the whole process remains straight talking and positive.

If at any time the client demonstrates an attitude of excuses and non co-operation they are eliminated from the programme. This may at first seem harsh, but the reality is that a busy hypnotherapist does not have endless time to spend looking at the reasons why the attitude is as it is. Don't get me wrong, the tone of the sessions is always positive and we work as a team to ensure that it continues so the motivation is strong.

Having been fat myself, I fully recognise that motivation fuels the determination to lose weight and ultimately the result on the scales. But at the end of the day you can take a horse to water but you cannot make it drink.

Does this mean I believe there are a small percentage of people who will prefer to live a lazy lifestyle and expect others to do the work for them? Yes. And those people have no place in my consulting room.

The Tools In Detail

The hypnotic script
You may be wondering what the hypnotic script actually is. In short this is literally a script of suggestions I use to embed in my client's unconscious mind. As previously mentioned each script is unique because clients' needs differ. Using a standard off the shelf script would potentially achieve nothing, so I always spend time tailoring it to the individual.

To help develop a script for the client I will ask a number of standard case history questions. The tone of the questions is very direct. Again the word 'fat' is used rather than softer language that does nothing but soften the motivation to lose weight. Here are some of the questions that I may ask a client:

1. What are your reasons for being fat?
2. What are the underlying reasons that have lead you to being fat?
3. What motivational techniques work best for you when losing weight?
4. What are your biggest fears if you remain too fat?
5. What do you see as your main challenge?
6. What are the solutions to helping you lose weight?
7. What is it that you want?
8. Do you accept that if the effort isn't put in you will simply stay fat?
9. What will you be able to do that you can't now once the fat has gone?
10. Do you accept there is no magic wand that will automatically make you melt the fat?

As you see, fact finding with a client is incredibly important and allows me the chance to develop a hypnotic script that is much more likely to generate a result. Let's take two examples. The first is a mini script and is developed for a client who reports that they are binge eating and need to regain control over food. The second mini script is tailored for a client who is reporting a lack of motivation and needs this ramped up as quickly as possible. In both examples let's imagine that I have installed a focused concentration in the client and their unconscious mind is now receptive to the suggestions.

Client reporting binge eating:-
You will from this immediate moment erase all mental programmes in your unconscious mind that lead you to binge eating. . .in fact the part that was responsible for binge eating has now been smashed. . .perhaps you can hear the smash and feel its intensity. . .what is for certain is that the trigger for binge eating is now smashed for good. . .you are now releasing any desire to binge. . .yes let it go now. . .cheer as it is released. . .you now have no desire to binge. . .you will from this moment have no desire to binge. . .I command this to your unconscious mind. . .binge eating is now well and truly in the past. . .and because you are binge free the fat is melting. . .yes the fat will continue to melt. . .you are now binge free. . .and when I awaken you. . .you will even forget that you were hypnotised. . .but you will immediately notice that something has changed. . .you will notice that a surge of control over your eating habits is in place. . .being fat is not an option for you any longer. . .you are now firmly in control of your eating habits. . .binge free for good. . .binge eating is smashed. . .obliterated. . .you are now binge free. . .

Client reporting a lack of motivation:-
You will automatically be aware that your motivation increases right now. . .because being fat is no longer for you. . .unlike fat people that choose to remain lazy and out of control you will

continue to drive your motivation forward. . .you will from this moment pay attention to the sadness of those who are fat because they are lazy and do nothing but moan about it. . .you know that life is not for you. . .and right now your unconscious mind will experience an increased motivation. . .and because of this and with no excuse. . .as you sit in the chair you experience the motivation running through every part of your body. . .all the way down to your feet. . .you know that fat will never win the day. . .you are too strong for that. . .of course you have a choice and that choice is to either stay fat. . .or become a healthy weight. . .you told me you wanted to look sexier. . .feel more confident. . .and for this reason you will right now. . .this minute. . .crank up your level of motivation. . .lift your head high. . .lift it higher. . .you are one of those that carries motivation. . .both inside and outside of this room. . .your motivation is now driving north. . .increase it right now. . .feels good doesn't it. . .

The 80-20 plan

It is of course important to provide a client with some guidance on a healthy way of eating. However given the confusion that is out there and nutritionists arguing amongst themselves as to what we should and should not eat, I provide my clients with a sensible and straightforward meal plan guide.

My 80-20 plan includes showing clients how they can build in a 'bit of what they fancy' each week so they understand they do not have to undertake a restricted diet.

Prior to seeing a client I may or may not ask them to keep a food diary so we can explore how their current eating habits need to change.

I always provide my six-week meal plan example for clients so that they can use it for guidance to develop their very own. As you will see each day incorporates the five a day best practice and is very practical. This menu plan is about balance and moderation; there are no banned foods. It's about eating less of some foods and more of others.

The basic rules
- Make sure you eat three meals a day with snacks twice daily.
- Stay hydrated, make water your drink of choice. Reduce intake of fizzy drinks and make sure you have between 6-8 glasses of water per day.
- Enjoy at least five fruits and vegetables a day. Remember a glass of juice counts as one of your five. Buy pure juice and not that 'from concentrated'.
- Reduce your alcohol intake and stay within weekly safe drinking limits.
- Cut out saturated fat found in pies, pasties, pastries, cakes and biscuits.
- Use a smaller plate to serve your lunch and dinner.
- Apply the 80-20 rule and eat healthy small portions 80% of the time. Use the portion control plate.
- Get active-build exercise into your daily routine. Check with the doctor first.
- Identify the foods you cannot live without and enjoy 'a little of what you fancy' occasionally! Remember portion control is key.

Motivational Tools

At the heart of my programme is motivation. Of course what works for one may not work for another so the tools are negotiated with the client. A range of motivational strategies are explored and may include:
- Hanging up an item of clothing that the client is desperate to fit into.

- Develop a series of Fat Warnings and posting these around the house.
- Designing a success chart on which a client can post their breakthroughs.
- Using a restaurant warning sign the client carries around that reads 'If you are fat, think before ordering'.
- Setting a variety of rewards for achievement of goals along the way.
- Taking up new hobbies and interests that fuel positive emotion into the client's life.

Steve Miller is the UK's renowned straight talking weight loss coach, hypnotherapist and media personality. He qualified as a clinical hypnotherapist sixteen years ago and is a Distinction Graduate of the London College of Clinical Hypnosis. Having struggled with his weight, Steve decided to niche in weight management and now runs a highly successful hypnotherapy practice where he works predominantly with clients struggling to lose and control their weight. Steve is also a published author, his latest book being Steve Miller's Slimming Secrets.

In 2010 Steve became the presenter of the hit TV show **Fat Families** *on Sky Living and went on to present 'Je Echte Leftijd' (Your Real Age) in the Netherlands. He is featured widely by the press and was recently branded; 'The Simon Cowell of the Slimming World'. There is not a month goes by without Steve and his success being featured. In 2014 he was appointed celebrity blogger to The Huffington Post and he is Hello Magazine's online weight loss expert. He delivers weight loss seminars teaching his audience how to use self hypnosis to achieve their ideal weight as well as supporting them develop a motivational plan to lose weight and keep it off.*

He is also Director of the Hypnotherapy Business School, the leading provider of business and marketing education for clinical hypnotherapists and is specialist advisor to the National Council for Hypnotherapy and a member of the British Society of Clinical Hypnosis.

Chapter Six

Dealing with phobias

Pat Duckworth describes the different types of phobia and how they originate and sets out how you can treat different types of phobia using a cognitive approach and neuro-linguistic programming techniques.

The definition of a phobia is "an irrational, obsessive, and intense fear that is focussed on a specific circumstance, idea or thing".

A significant proportion of the population, around 70 per cent, experience mild phobic responses and about 20 per cent of those have a serious enough issue to fit the above definition. Common phobias include fear of spiders, snakes, heights, dogs, thunder and lightning, injections, flying and germs or dirt. However people can become phobic about almost anything. I have dealt with a client with a fear of black barns and I know of people with phobias of polka dots and loose buttons.

Phobias are part of the fight or flight response to things and situations that the brain perceives as a danger. The sufferer's brain is working perfectly well, but the alarm system has been set up too sensitively and is triggered when it is inappropriate. The fear can become generalised from the initial trigger into a range of similar objects or situations.

For example, an incident with a bee sting can develop into a phobia of bees which then becomes a bee and wasp phobia and then a fear of anything that flies and makes a buzzing sound. I even had a client whose bee phobia was triggered by the buzzing sound of a small motorbike engine.

Where do phobias come from?

There are a number of theories about how phobias develop. Some phobias develop from a single significant negative emotional event connected with the thing that is feared. The response then becomes a learned behaviour. Other phobias may develop from anxieties arising in childhood. These can be exacerbated by reinforcement of the anxiety by parents.

The cognitive approach suggests that phobias may also develop from distorted thoughts about the thing feared. For example, a person in a crowded underground train which stops in a tunnel may think: "I might suffocate if I get trapped in this train." This leads to a fear of the underground which could then get generalised into similar situations such as lifts and tunnels. The sufferer may then develop claustrophobia.

Types of phobia

Psychologists divide phobias into three categories:
• Simple or Specific Phobias – fear of a specific object or situation, for example; spiders, snakes, flying heights, claustrophobia
• Agoraphobia – literally fear of the market place but essentially a fear of everything outside of a defined safe environment. Often this has a social phobia at its root.
• Social Phobia – fear of social situations and interaction with other people. Often involves a fear of others' opinions, for example; exams, public speaking, meetings. These feelings may have a root in fear or failure, rejection, disapproval or not being loved.

What is a phobic response

The phobic response is a complex interaction between brain chemistry, environmental triggers and learned behaviour. Research into the development of phobias has been carried out by giving students electric shocks when they were exposed to certain stimuli such as snakes, tomatoes, guns and knives. They could all develop a phobic response after only a few shocks. This demonstrates how quickly we can learn a phobic response depending on the intensity and timing of the negative experience associated with exposure to the object.

This experiment also illustrated that people are more likely to develop a phobic reaction to some stimuli rather than others. Many more people have phobias about spiders and snakes than cars even though they are much less likely to suffer harm from insects and reptiles. It is argued that this is a result of psychological predisposition to be sensitive to objects that were sources of danger to us thousands of years ago when our brain structures were developing (Seligman, 1971).

A phobia is different from a strong dislike of something. For example, someone with a strong dislike of spiders will want to kill one when they see it or remove it from the room. Somebody with a phobia will be unable to take their eyes off of the spider once they spot it and will probably be unable to go anywhere near it in order to deal with it.

A phobic response is characterised by:
- Avoidance behaviour – the client will try to avoid places or circumstances where the phobia could be triggered.
- Hyper-vigilance – the client will be watching for the object of their fear to appear.

There will also be a physical response which may include:
- Heightened heart rate or palpitations
- Rapid breathing or breathlessness

- Sweating
- Nausea
- Dizziness

These physical responses are the result of the release of certain hormones into the bloodstream. When the alarm reaction is triggered by the object or situation, the body responds with a drop in blood pressure and muscle tension. This is followed by an alerting response in which cortisol and adrenaline are released into the system. Glucose is released from the liver to provide fuel for quick energy. Muscles are tensed in preparation for running away.

If the phobic response is triggered regularly it will cause wear and tear on the sufferer's system. Muscles become fatigued and the person may become more prone to infections and illnesses.

From the NLP perspective, a phobia is a classic example of a faulty neuro-linguistic program. The NLP approach to treating phobias brings together aspects of helping the client to alter their thinking about the thing they fear with dealing with traumas which may have been suppressed. The most effective way to address the faulty program is to interrupt or destabilise it and then install a new response.

One of the main ways to treat phobias using NLP is by interrupting the phobic pattern using V-K dissociation or 'The Fast Phobia Cure'. V-K dissociation involves separating the client's visual experience (V) from their feelings or kinaesthetic response (K).

Through double dissociation and changing the sub-modalities of the memory of the phobia, the client can watch their earlier behaviour and change their reaction to the phobic stimulus. In some cases, additional techniques are required. If the client has a general level of anxiety that preceded the phobia, Time Line Reframing (TLR) can enable the client to explore other choices and reactions to the original stimulus of their anxiety.

In one case a client came to me to deal with her growing fear of horse riding, an activity that she had previously enjoyed. The fear appeared to be related to a bad experience of being thrown from a horse.

However, during the initial session it became obvious that she was experiencing an underlying level of anxiety. I used TLR on her feeling of anxiety and she went back to the death of her grandparents several years earlier. After she reframed that experience, the horse related incidents became insignificant. She felt able to remember happy, resourceful times with her grandmother and she reported feeling generally more confident and positive.

Your first contact with a phobic client

Many people live with their phobias because at some level the fear appears to them to be rational and the phobia is protecting them from the object or situation. They tend to seek help when the phobia has started to seriously impact on their lives or they get fed up with being afraid.

Be cautious of dealing with a client who tells you that someone else thought it was a good idea for them to get help with their phobia.

If it was not their idea to contact you, they may not buy into the process and the chances of success are severely diminished. To gauge their commitment, ask them to indicate on a scale of one to ten how motivated they are to get over their phobia. If they are at a six or below, you will need to ask more questions about what would increase their motivation.

Some clients will contact you because there is an event approaching that is connected with their phobia and often that event is very close.

For example I have had a client who wanted me to help her

overcome her dog phobia before she visited a friend two days later and another client who wanted me to sort out her daughter's stage fright before a performance on the following evening! The good news is that in both cases I was able to treat the phobias effectively.

It is a good idea to ask whether they have any other phobias. This will reveal whether they have a general background level of anxiety which may require additional therapy.

The client may ask how many sessions the treatment is likely to involve. Some simple/specific phobias may only require two one-hour sessions or one two-hour session. However, you need to add a caveat that you will not know how many sessions will be required until you start working together.

If the client has an event coming up soon which would involve the phobia, suggest that they see you as soon as possible for a longer session. This will give them and you the best chance of success.

Agoraphobia and social phobias are likely to require more sessions. It is difficult to predict the number of sessions required because it will depend on the root cause and complexity of the phobia. You could indicate the average number of sessions that you normally have with clients which for me would be between two and six sessions.

If your client is agoraphobic they may, initially, be unable to leave their own home. In extreme cases they may be confined to just one room. In that case the initial session will be at the client's property and you will need to ask about the facilities and whether they can guarantee that you will not be disturbed during the therapy. You may wish to include travel time and mileage in your fee.

The client may ask about your success rate. You cannot guarantee success, but you can say that fears and phobias are generally very responsive to NLP techniques and hypnotherapy.

The First Session

Before you see your client for the first time, think about the therapy environment. I know it may seem obvious, but think about whether there is anything in or around your therapy room that might trigger the phobia. Are there any objects or images or sounds that might represent the object of fear to the client? If they have a fear of heights, are they able to walk up stairs? Remember, the client will be hyper-vigilant and scanning the environment.

Client history
During the first session for all three types of phobias you will be completing a client history or intake form. The information you require is:

A brief description of their phobia(s)
- When did it start? Was there a specific event that triggered it?
- Is there a threshold for the phobia (e.g. size of spider, height of building, size of aircraft?)
- Are there times when they don't have their phobic response?
- Are there times when it is better?
- Are there times when it is worse?
- Is there anything they believe about their phobia (e.g. their mother was always anxious; they know that it is irrational or rational)?

What starts the phobic response?
- What is in the environment?
- Is it a certain time before an event?
- Is there a thought that they have?
- Where does the feeling start?
- What are the physical sensations that they experience?

- What are the sub-modalities of the fear? If it had a colour, what colour would it be? If it had a shape, size, weight or temperature what would that be?
- What happens next? What do they do in response to the phobia? What do they do to control it?
- What needs to happen for the response to finish?
- How do they feel when the episode is finished?

If the client has more than one simple/specific phobia ask them to rate the importance of each one on a scale of 1-10. Which one would it be most helpful to deal with first? Dealing with one phobia may have a knock-on effect to the other phobias.

I always record a relaxation/hypnotic track for my clients after the first appointment, even for simple/specific phobias that appear to have been dealt with. The recording helps to consolidate the work that you have done and carry on the relaxation process. Some clients are reassured by having a recording that they can use before any interaction with their phobic object or situation.

Future pacing

In order to put together a script for that recording, you need to know how the client wants their life to be without their phobia. You are future pacing their perfect outcome. You can find out this information using questions based around Neuro-Logical Levels and ask how things will be when the client does not have this phobia any more.

Ask the client:

- Environment – Where will you be? What will be around you? What will you see, hear and feel?
- Behaviour – What will you be doing? What actions will you be taking?
- Capabilities – What strengths and resources do you already have that will help you to get over this problem? What strengths

and resources do you need?
- Beliefs – What can you believe about yourself with this phobia gone?
- Values – What is important in your life? What motivates you?
- Identity – Who are you without your phobia?
- Purpose – "If you had a purpose, a reason to be on this earth, what would it be?" (Silvester, 2003)

Solution focus
Alternatively, you could use the 'Solutions Focus' approach (Jackson & McKergow, 2002). You can ask the client:

'Suppose that tonight you go to bed, and you go to sleep as usual, and during the night a miracle happens and the phobia vanishes, but you're asleep so you don't know that the miracle has happened. So when you wake up tomorrow, what will be the first thing that will tell you that the miracle has happened? How will you know that the transformation has occurred?' Elicit a long list of how the client will know that the phobia has gone.

Therapy Structure

Simple or specific phobias
For a simple or specific phobia one session may be all that it needed. I have got rid of a 20-year phobia in just 15 minutes. In Session 1, I carry out a history take and future pace the perfect outcome for the client. In this session or the next, according to the individual needs of the client I may use a Fast Phobia Cure and hypnosis to reinforce this. I will also give the client a relaxation/hypnotic recording.

Steps in the Fast Phobia Cure (V-K Dissociation)
Step 1
Ask the client to identify the incident relating to the phobic response (if the client is unable to identify a first event connected

with the phobia, you may have to use the Time Line Reframing technique detailed below to help them find that event.)

Step 2
Ask the client to visualise a blank cinema screen in front of them, as if they are sitting in the cinema. Then ask them to float back to the projection room so that they are looking at themselves looking at the cinema screen (double dissociated).

Step 3
Ask the client to put on the screen an image of the moment before the incident started so that they are feeling safe. Now freeze that image and turn it black and white.

Step 4
Ask the client to close their eyes, if they haven't already, and run the incident forward on the screen all the way through until they are feeling safe at the other end of it. Allow them to take all of the time they need. You can talk quietly in the background saying things like: "That's right, letting the film run all the way through until safe at the other end. All the time you need." Watch their physiology while they are doing it. If they start to look overly distressed, suggest that they move the screen further away until they feel comfortable.

Step 5
When the client indicates that they are at the end at the safe place, ask them to turn the image into colour and then move up into the film so that they are now looking at it through their own eyes (associated). Now run the movie backwards as quickly as they can, seeing the whole event in reverse until they are safe at the beginning. You may want to make a 'zip' sound or click your fingers to encourage speed.

Step 6
Break state and then repeat steps 3 to 5 several more times. Notice any changes in the time it takes for the client to run the film forward and any changes in their physiology. Ask them,

between cycles, what they are noticing that is changing. Has there been any change in what they are thinking about the event? Once they start to relax you can add a 'sound track' to Step 5 by singing a funny tune while they wind the film backwards, for example the Benny Hill tune or a circus tune. Finally you can ask them to join in singing the tune while they watch the film of the event running backwards.

There is another step that you can add once the client reports having new understandings about the event. You can ask them to run the movie forward again with the new learning and understanding while they watch in the cinema.

Once the client confirms that they can think about the thing that used to trigger their phobia without any adverse response, it may be appropriate to ask them if they want to test the improvement through some sort of controlled exposure to the trigger. For example, if they arrived with a fear of dogs, you may want to take them for a walk until you see a dog. Note their reaction and assess whether any more work is required.

You can finish the session with an induction and some hypnotic messages to reinforce the work you have done.

Agoraphobia & Social Phobias

It often takes longer to deal with these phobias. A four session programme could look like this:

Session 1:
- History take and future perfect

Session 2:
- Time Line Reframing
- Fast Phobia Cure
- Hypnosis to reinforce fast phobia cure
- Relaxation/hypnotic recording

Session 3:
- Review what is working
- More TLR on negative emotions
- Anchoring a positive emotion
- Drop Through negative emotions
- Relaxation techniques

Session 4:
- Review what is working
- Swish
- Theatre of the Mind
- Change Link positive changes

Time Line Reframing

Time Line Reframing (TLR) is a technique for reframing negative experiences that have happened in the past. Before you use TLR with a client, it is helpful to explain the background to the technique. I normally explain that memories are stored in one part of the brain and while they are there, they are set in concrete and do not change. In order to remember them, we move them to a different part of the brain, and, once they are there they become plastic and you can make changes to them. Metaphors like files in a filing cabinet or electronic files in the computer memory can be helpful.

I then explain that once the memory is plastic, you can add new learning into it and the memory that goes back into storage will be more helpful. The unconscious can now react in a different way to the situation that used to trigger the phobia.

I also explain to the client that however long ago the event occurred, they know more now than they did then. So there is always something that the client now can help their younger self to understand.

The process of recalling a previous trauma may provoke an

abreaction that is 'a release of emotional tension'. If the client appears to be overly distressed you can instruct them to move higher above their TL to a safe distance from the event or take whatever action seems appropriate to them to be able to observe the memory safely.

For example, some clients may want to view the scene from behind a screen. If they are still distressed ask them to open their eyes and break state.

The steps in Time Line Reframing

Step 1

Set up the client's time line. 'If you could imagine a line that connects your past to your future, where would you point to your past? Where would your future be? And if the line had a colour, what colour would it be. If you can't see that line, do you get a sense or feeling of it?

Now if I was to ask you to be above that line, would you move above it or would it move away from you? And if I wanted you to move along that line, would you move or would the line move underneath you?'

At this stage I often do a 'test flight' by asking the client to move above their TL and move out to an event in the near future that they know is going to happen and look down into that event. I check that they can do that and then bring them back to now and being in the chair.

Step 2

Identify the first event. Ask the client to close their eyes and move or float above their TL and from that position ask their unconscious mind if there was a first event connected to that feeling of (fear/anxiety/panic) so that by going back to it they could let it go completely and for good, when was that event? Some clients may have problems identifying the event and you can encourage them by saying: "And it may not be the first event, it is just the first event that you remember now". When they say that they have the event you can ask how old they were in that event. Then ask them to allow their unconscious mind to float back along their TL all the way back to that event until they are above it and can look down and see what is going on. Ask them if it is OK for them to share the details with you and, if so, ask them to share the details.

Step 3

Establish the connection and the learning. Ask the client: "If there was a connection between that event and the (fear /anxiety/panic) that you have had up until now, what would that connection be?" Once they have made the connection they can start to identify what they know now that they didn't know then.

Ask the client: "If there was something you at that age could learn from you now, that by learning it would mean he/she could let go of that feeling completely and for good, what would you have him/her learn?" Keep asking this question until the client says there is nothing else. Then invite them, in whatever way they would imagine doing it, to pass all that learning down to their younger self. Check that the younger person has received that learning.

Step 4

Check that there isn't an earlier event connected with the phobia. Ask the client to move along their TL to just before the event occurred so that they are looking towards the future and they can look down at the event as though it below and in front of them.

Ask them if from that position the negative feeling has gone. If it has gone you can go to Step 5. If it hasn't gone, ask them: "If there was an earlier event connected to that feeling, you can ask your unconscious mind, now, to go back to that event." You then repeat Steps 3 and 4.

Step 5
Associate with the memory. Once the client reports that the feeling has gone, you can ask them whether it would be okay to go down into the event and notice that the feeling has gone and how different the situation is. They may even want to hug their younger self.

Step 6
Bring back the learning. Instruct the client to float back above their TL imagining the difference it would have made for their younger self to grow free from the old emotion.

Then ask them to come back along their TL, bringing with them all the learning, and noticing along the way any other events that used to be connected to the old emotion and what more they can learn that means they can let go of the effects of the old feeling.

Step 7
Future pacing. Ask the client to imagine moving along their TL to an event in the future which, if it had happened in the past would have been connected to that feeling they used to have. Once they are above that event, ask them what is different about it. When they report that it is better ask them to notice all the differences in what they can see, hear and feel that means that they are thinking differently about it.

Then ask them to imagine going down into that event and looking through the eyes of themselves in the future so they can see how they want to be.

Finally, ask them to bring all of that learning back to now while you continue to give them reinforcing messages about noticing all of the positive changes that they can notice from today.

The client may not be able to reframe the experience in Step 3 because there are no positive interpretations. You may need to take them through the Fast Phobia Cure on that event instead.

Techniques and phrases for a hypnotic script

Due to the variety of phobias and client experiences, it is not helpful to provide a generic script. However there are some phrases that you could include:

• And whatever is the first small thing you notice that means that you are letting go of that feeling you in your (head/chest/stomach) no longer need to have. . .
• Because now you know that the old way of thinking served a purpose, keeping you safe. . .but now there are better ways of getting on with your life. . .
• Isn't it nice to know that you already have all the resources within you to let go of this problem because sometimes you have to let go and when you let go something even better can happen. . .
• And you might be surprised the first time you notice that you were somewhere doing something and you knew that you were feeling calm/confident/relaxed. . .
• And we all have hundreds and thousands of thoughts every day. . .and some are negative and some are positive. . .some are limiting and some are enabling. . .and what matters is which thoughts we pay attention to. . .and you can find yourself. . .more and more. . .noticing the positive thoughts. . .
• And I'm not saying that it's easy, only that it's possible and in the days and weeks ahead you can notice more and more. . .
• Maybe you haven't thought, yet, of all the ways you can enjoy your life so much more, free from that old thinking. . .
• You may have already started to notice the changes in how you think/feel about that thing that used to worry you and that means those positive changes can continue over the coming days and weeks and months, until it just becomes normal that you no longer have the problem you used to have. . .

- And you can imagine yourself a few weeks from now and you have been listening to your recording regularly, practising (relaxing breathing/anchoring/positive visualisation), letting go of old ways of thinking. Thinking about yourself in more positive ways and feeling and how good does that feel?. . .
- And you might forget to remember the problem you used to have. . .

REFERENCES

Dilts, R. & DeLozier, J (2000) Encyclopedia of Systemic NLP and NLP New Coding, *NLP University Press*

Jackson, P.Z. (2002) The Solutions Focus; Making Coaching & Change SIMPLE, *Nicholas Brealey International*

Seligman, M.E.P. (1971) Phobias and preparedness. Behavior Therapy, 2, 307 – 320

Silvester, T. (2003) Wordweaving Volume 1; The Science of Suggestion, *The Quest Institute*

Pat Duckworth MBA, NLP Master Prac., Dip CHyp., HPD., is a Cognitive Hypnotherapist, award winning author and trainer.

Pat sees clients on a one-to-one basis at her therapy rooms in Harley Street, London, Cambridgeshire and Toronto. She specialises in helping women experiencing menopause symptoms including hot flushes, weight gain, poor sleep, loss of confidence and mood swings.

Pat has designed and delivered training and workshops on a wide range of well-being subjects and is a sought after public-speaker. She is a regular guest on BBC Radio Cambridgeshire. She has had a series of articles published by **The Hypnotherapy Journal.**

In 2012 she published **Hot Women, Cool Solutions; How to control menopause symptoms using mind/body techniques,** *followed by* **How to Survive Her Menopause; A practical guide to women's health for men** *in 2013. She has also contributed to* **Your 101 Ways to 101** *by Dr George Grant and* **The Planet of Wellness** *by Marina Nani.*

Her latest book is **Cool Recipes for Hot Women; How to eat your way to a healthy menopause**, *with leading nutritionist Jenny Tschieshe, published in June 2014*

Pat is a consultant to the CAM Fertility Centre and to the Active Mum programme.

Chapter Seven

An overview of pain

Clem Turner describes how pain can affect many aspects of well being. He shows how the client's own resources for dealing with pain can be utilised and developed using hypnotherapy.

Pain is something we all experience at sometime in our life. Physical pain is a feeling that lets your brain know something is wrong with your body. It sends a warning message which can be felt as discomfort, tingling, burning, throbbing, stabbing, soreness, aching or sometimes agony. Unless we have pain we simply wouldn't be aware that there is a problem somewhere in our body and we need to do something about it.

Pain is a very individual experience and can only be described by the person experiencing it. What is pain or painful to you may not be to someone else.

Pain can be mild or severe or anything in between. There can be thousands of causes for pain and many times you may not know the cause. Sometimes the cause of pain is obvious such as a broken arm or severe bruising, but when pain is internal it can be difficult to establish the exact cause.

Sometimes habits are created by being in pain, these could be low moods, inactivity, comfort eating, focusing on the pain or having panic attacks.

The textbook explanation of pain is: an unpleasant sensory and emotional experience associated with actual or potential tissue damage.

Unfortunately, millions of people face this problem on a regular basis, and living with pain can seriously affect the quality of life of anyone who is forced to endure it.

Pain Statistics

It is believed that between 8 and 10 million people in the UK suffer pain almost on a daily basis, this naturally results in regular days off work and has a major impact on their quality of life. It is thought that there are around 208 million working days lost through pain each year.

Looking at the bigger picture it is estimated that 120 million adults worldwide suffer from pain.

Types of pain
Acute pain
Acute pain can be short-lived but intense at the time. It usually comes on suddenly, sometimes lasting hours or days. It may occur after surgery, illness or an injury; but when the body heals, the pain usually subsides. Think of it like an alarm telling us something is wrong with the body, this then motivates the person to get help. Acute pain is beneficial to the patient because if it wasn't for the pain, the individual would ignore his or her illness which could result in complications or serious consequences. Examples of acute pain would include:
- Heart attack
- Acute appendicitis
- Bone fracture
- Muscle sprain
- Displaced disc in the spine

Chronic or persistent pain
Longer term pain is called chronic or persistent pain. The severity of chronic pain can vary from mild to excruciating and can be ongoing or relentless, lasting for weeks, months or even years.

Chronic pain might be caused by an initial trauma or injury or there might be ongoing causes of pain.

Examples of chronic pain would include:
- Tendonitis
- Carpal tunnel syndrome
- Joint or back pain
- Osteo and rheumatoid arthritis
- Shingles

This type of pain not only causes the sufferer physical and mental stress, but it can weaken their immune system and slow down the healing process.

It can also cause fatigue which affects ability to go to work or socialise and can also affect sleep pattern. Continuing pain can bring about emotional changes such as mood swings, depression or irritability.

Emotional Pain
Pain isn't always caused through physical trauma; it can be caused by emotional and/or mental distress.

Feelings of loss, guilt, rejection, a hurtful remark from a friend or being lonely can all cause a client to feel pain. Feelings of anxiety and stress can also worsen such painful syndromes as Irritable Bowel Syndrome and fibromyalgia.

Referred Pain
Also known as reflective pain, this is a pain which is felt at a location other than the actual site of the pain. An example of this would be a heart attack where the pain is often felt in the

neck, shoulders and the left arm rather than in the chest which is the site of the trauma.

Other characteristics of pain

Sometimes the pain system can get confused and work too efficiently or not at all.

Phantom limb pain is the pain that is felt in the part of the body which has been amputated, for example an arm or a leg. The brain misinterprets the nerve signals as coming from the amputated limb. The phantom limb pain is described as squeezing, burning, or a crushing sensation, and it often differs from any sensation previously experienced by the patient.

Some life threatening illnesses like cancer can cause the patient no pain at all in the initial stages which means they are unaware of any problems with their health, sometimes until it is too late. Conversely some non life-threatening issues like gout or toothache cause acute pain to the sufferer.

Sometimes pain can be put on hold. An example of this might be a soldier who is injured on the battlefield and because of the rush of adrenaline, which kills the pain temporarily he is able to escape from the danger until it's safe for him to feel the pain. Another example might be a professional sports person who suffers an injury whilst taking part in a race, but once again the adrenaline kicks in and they continue without feeling pain, sometimes causing even more injury to themselves.

Types of Pain Relief

The body is constantly being damaged and symptoms can go unnoticed. We human beings have survived for hundreds of thousands of years without medicine but, in contemporary society, the first method people generally use is to go to their doctor and get a prescription for pain relief.

The doctor will probably prescribe tablets but may also suggest creams and gels to rub onto the affected area or an injection directly into the site of pain. Unfortunately, some patients become addicted to medication and there is a possibility that in the long term medication may stop working altogether as the body becomes used to it.

Most medication carries side effects. These side effects can in turn cause more problems which can lead to more medication being prescribed and a vicious circle developing. In extreme cases doctors may suggest surgery to be the best method of cure.

Of course, in many cases medication is effective. For example, a recent breakthrough has found that up to 40 per cent of chronic back pain sufferers can be cured with a course of antibiotics as some back pain can be caused by previously unknown bacteria.

Other methods of pain relief

There are many other methods of pain relief, visiting an osteopath or chiropractor if the problem is skeletal for example. The difference between the two professions is that chiropractors make sure the body is working optimally to prevent any disease and osteopaths treat the symptoms with which the patient presents. Both treat the body with a safe, natural and drug-free method of health care.

In many cases bad posture can be the cause of pain and a trip to a bio-mechanic practitioner can be very helpful as they teach people good posture and can suggest exercises that will improve posture in the future.

If the pain is muscular it is now widely accepted that acupuncture can help. Acupuncture has been used for over 2,000 years to help a variety of different health problems and recently the National Institute for Health and Clinical Excellence (NICE) decided that acupuncture could be made available on the NHS for chronic lower back.

Heat treatment such as a heat pad or hot water bottle can promote healing as it increases blood flow to the painful area and will also help muscles to relax.

Similarly, cold treatments such as an ice pack restrict the blood flow and can reduce swelling.

Exercise, even in its simplest form such as stretching, also increases blood flow which helps bring healing fluids to the site of pain. Having a gentle massage has a similar affect, helping muscles to relax or just gentling rubbing the area of pain can have a soothing effect.

Over recent years there has been an increase in the use of certain electrical machines such as tens machines to help with pain. These machines help to block the nerves carrying the pain.

Other methods of reducing pain can include non-prescription or over the counter medications, which are widely available.

When a person has been in chronic pain the original problem may have abated, but the neurology has not been turned off, therefore the pain can outlive its usefulness. Therefore the pain needs to be stopped, but rarely do people look to themselves in an attempt to control it. It's almost as though we have been conditioned to accept that we need someone or something external to make the pain go away.

Using our own resources

And yet real pain relief and effective pain control can be found within the sufferer's own inner resources. To understand that we have the resources within our self to control pain is a major step forward in releasing its truly debilitating grip on our life.

By using hypnotherapy, and the other treatments and therapies such as: Neuro-Linguistic-Programming (NLP);

Emotional Freedom Technique (EFT); Eye Movement Desensitization and Reprogramming (EMDR); and Hypno Cognitive Behavioural Therapy (HCBT) the client can instruct their own mind to dramatically reduce, and in many cases totally eliminate any pain they may be experiencing.

How hypnotherapy works for pain management

Hypnotherapy has been used for many years to manage different types of pain including joint pain, Irritable Bowel Syndrome, sciatica and also pain from injuries and illnesses.

Hypnotherapy for pain management can be used either alone or alongside medication but if a person is considering using hypnotherapy for pain control they should visit their doctor for a diagnosis before proceeding. This is important to eliminate more serious causes of pain – for example the root cause of a persistent headache could possibly be a brain tumour, which a medical professional would be able to diagnose.

The hypnotherapist needs to be aware that sometimes it is right to remove pain and sometimes it is not. The pain the sufferer is feeling might be necessary, it might be there as a warning to the person that they need to find out what is wrong and get a correct diagnosis. If the pain is taken away the person might sustain further injury which might worsen the condition.

An example of when it would not be right to remove all pain would be a broken bone because releasing the pain may cause the client to forget about the bone being broken and be tempted to use it which would ultimately cause more damage.

However, in some cases it is right to go ahead and remove pain, as the pain is not necessary and its absence will not cause the patient further problems. Examples of this would be pain caused by dental work, phantom limb pain, childbirth, terminal illness, shingles and surgery.

Hypnotherapy changes the way the client responds to the pain signal, and practising mindfulness meditation creates a positive internal focus and changes negative beliefs. In some cases it can create more effective responses to medication by stimulating the brain's analgesic response.

There are many suggestions the hypnotherapist can make to the client, these could include somatic metaphor, glove anaesthesia or changing the pain to a different sensation, to name but a few.

Initial Consultation

At the initial consultation it is of paramount importance to build up rapport with the client. Quite often they have been told by the medical profession that there is nothing that can be done and they will have to put up with the pain. Many clients have already been to pain clinics and the hypnotherapist is the last resort. It is our job to change their belief system and make them realise that by using their own natural resources with our help, they can remove pain completely if it is unnecessary pain, and bring necessary pain down to a manageable level.

The initial contact

Firstly the client should fill in a consent form, together with a comprehensive form establishing various aspects of his or her pain issues, such as the history of the pain, the intensity, the type, the cause and importantly what the pain prevents them from doing and what they will be able to do once the pain is manageable or gone. It is also useful to record what they want and what they expect from the treatments they are about to undertake.

Quite often clients are suffering from anxiety, caused by the attrition associated with long-term pain; therefore it would be a good idea to check the client's anxiety levels before commencing treatment. It is also useful to discuss the approximate number of treatments required and of course the cost of these treatments.

It is essential to point out that you will work together as a team and once you have designed a treatment plan specifically for them, they must fulfil their obligations and commitment by practising coping skills and listening to CDs between sessions.

It is important to remember that no one treatment fits all – this is why the hypnotherapist needs to have a variety of different treatments at their disposal.

Diet, lifestyle and pain

It is important to establish whether the client has a healthy diet and a healthy lifestyle as all of the following can contribute to pain:
- Poor diet
- Too much caffeine
- Too much sugar
- Being overweight
- Excess alcohol
- Smoking or drug taking
- Lack of exercise
- Poor quality sleep
- No time to rest and relax
- Inability to say 'No' to other people

Dealing with the healthy eating issue first of all, it is essential that the client has a good balanced diet which is necessary for healing, general wellbeing, an efficient immune system and also for the management of pain.

A balanced diet should include protein for tissue repair and carbohydrates for energy, and the client would benefit from eating fruit and vegetables regularly.

Consuming a diet that is rich in antioxidants may be helpful for the relief of chronic pain. Illnesses like rheumatoid arthritis and fibromyalgia could benefit from eating foods like cherries, oranges, peaches, asparagus, cranberries, kiwi and cauliflower. Dairy products, chocolate, eggs and meat can sometimes worsen inflammation in rheumatoid arthritis.

The right liquids
As well as getting your client on the right track as far as eating is concerned, it is also important to encourage them to drink plenty of water.

Chronic pains such as arthritis pain, angina, lower back pain, migraine and colitis pain are commonly the result of chronic dehydration and if we are just 2 per cent dehydrated our bodies cannot function efficiently.

There are many theories about how much water we should drink but in his book called *Your Body's Many Cries for Water* Dr Batmanghelidj recommends that we should drink a minimum of six to eight, eight ounce glasses of water every day. He also maintains that in many cases people are not sick, they're dehydrated.

Drinking water is one of the best methods of relieving fluid retention. When the body is dehydrated it perceives this as a threat to survival and begins to hold onto every drop which shows up in swollen feet, hands and legs. Diuretics only offer a temporary solution because they force out stored water along with some essential nutrients which again the body perceives as a threat and will replace the lost water at the first opportunity. The best way to overcome the problem of water retention is to give your body what it needs – plenty of water – and then the stored water will be released.

Check that your client is not drinking lots of caffeine either in coffee, tea or fizzy drinks.

Caffeine is a drug that is naturally produced in the leaves and seeds of many plants. It is defined as a drug because it stimulates the central nervous system, causing increased alertness and gives some people a temporary energy boost and elevated mood.

However, caffeine can also aggravate certain heart problems and can interact badly with some medications or supplements. If a person is stressed or anxious caffeine can make these feelings worse and in extreme cases can cause severe headaches or shaking. Health conditions that can be aggravated by caffeine include:

- Heart disease including high blood pressure, and high cholesterol
- Acid reflux
- Women's health problems such as pre-menstrual syndrome, menopausal symptoms, infertility, and osteoporosis
- Diabetes
- Irritable Bowel Syndrome, Crohn's Disease and Colitis
- Cystitis
- Sleeplessness and fatigue
- Stress
- Mood disorders and depression
- Migraine headaches

Instead of your client drinking caffeinated tea and coffee you should encourage them to drink more water, herbal or green tea. They will soon be noticing a positive effect in many areas of their lives.

Some people are tempted to turn to alcohol for pain relief and because alcohol does have the ability to suppress the nervous system, it can indeed give a certain amount of relief. However, the body begins to build up a tolerance to the effects of alcohol and it then takes more alcohol to produce the same results.

Naturally over time this can cause more health problems including stomach ulcers or life threatening liver disease.

Those people who drink excessive amounts of alcohol and take drugs, even over the counter medication, can find that because alcohol and certain drugs don't mix well they can cause severe negative side effects, for example alcohol and aspirin can damage the stomach lining and alcohol and ibuprofen can cause stomach ulcers and bleeding. Therefore, it is not a good plan to drink alcohol whilst taking medication.

If your client is a smoker this can also mean they will ultimately experience more pain. It is known that nicotine reduces the efficiency of the heart and lungs in delivering oxygen to the body. It also reduces the skin's elasticity, increases heart rate and blood pressure and it slows down the healing process. In conclusion, cigarettes not only weaken your health but they can intensify the feelings of pain.

The importance of exercise and sleep
When a person is in pain there is a temptation to avoid exercise, but it can often help to improve the quality of life. In some cases exercise can assist in reducing the pain and used correctly can release endorphins which cause the person to feel better.

Sometimes when people are in pain they try to guard themselves against the pain by limping. They might also put a strain on other parts of their body in their effort not to feel the pain. However, a muscle which is unused can go into spasm which can result in pain being increased and ultimately an unused muscle can atrophy or waste away.

Most people are capable of doing some form of exercise and it's not necessary to join a gym or run a marathon to keep fit and healthy. Low impact exercises such as walking, swimming, Pilates, yoga or tai chi or just simple stretching exercises will definitely help the client feel the benefit.

Sometimes when a person is in pain or anxious about something it can interfere with sleep patterns and it is essential that the client is encouraged to practice good sleep hygiene such as limiting caffeine and alcohol and getting more exercise.

In my experience if a client has a poor quality of sleep it is an advantage to teach breathing techniques and self hypnosis. This encourages the client to have a more positive mental attitude which in turn promotes better quality sleep. Listening to a relaxation CD (which you can record and produce yourself) is also helpful to promote sleep for the client. The main reason for giving a client a CD to listen to is to consolidate the suggestions given in the therapy room. It also makes the client have some 'me' time which is vitally important and after the sessions are completed they can go back to them at any time. I also give a client an information pack on pain and the types of pain and how hypnotherapy and other treatments can help them.

However, as much as we want to help the client, we need to be aware that we cannot help everyone, so at the end of the initial consultation be prepared if necessary to refer clients back to doctors, chiropractors, osteopaths, acupuncturists or other health professionals if you feel that your treatments are not suitable for the particular client or you feel the client has needs which are outside your sphere of capability.

Hypnotherapy Sessions
First session
At the start of this session I usually check the pain levels as progress should always be monitored throughout the treatment to establish when the sessions should terminate. Also at this session I would teach a coping skill such as glove anaesthesia and it may also be helpful to the client to learn a breathing exercise.

The hypnotherapy on this session concentrates on giving the client the confidence that the treatment will be successful and that their lives will improve as the body starts to heal.

At the end of that session I give the client a CD to listen to at home.

Second Session
Always discuss with the client what progress has been made and check their pain levels. The second session of hypnotherapy includes suggestions for releasing negative emotion and thoughts and concentrating on the positive aspect of life. At this session I would teach a coping technique such as thought stopping and if I think it necessary would give the client a confidence trigger.

Other useful techniques this session could be teaching the client to change the colour of the pain and melt it away.

At the end of this session I would once again give the client a CD to listen to at home.

Third Session
Once again check the pain levels and discuss progress over the previous week. At this session I would teach the client self hypnosis and explain the importance of positive affirmations. The hypnotherapy session this week encourages the client to think about the future without pain.

Any subsequent sessions
Any further sessions would depend very much on the progress you have been making with the client, but if you feel that insufficient progress has been made it could be that the client has a blockage towards progress being made. There are a number of issues that can block progress with a client including

- Self sabotage
- Secondary gain
- Unresolved emotional issues
- Lack of belief that they can be helped
- Fear of failure
- Anger
- Guilt

- Food intolerance

Establishing what the blockages are can be complicated and I am unable to go into details in this chapter. However I do go into this in some detail on my Pain Management Workshop. Methods of dealing with blockages could be any of the following treatments:
- NLP
- EFT
- Regression to cause
- EMDR
- Ideo-motor
- Psychological reversal
- Parts therapy
- Time line therapy
- Collapsing anchors
- Noesitherapy

Always remember, you cannot help everyone, never regard this as a failure on your behalf just accept that the client may need more specialist treatment that you are able to offer.

If this subject particularly interests you and you would like to read more about it the following books will be very useful to you:

REFERENCES
Hypnotherapy *Dave Elman*
Hartland's Medical and Dental Hypnosis *Michael Heap*
Hypnosis in the Relief of Pain *Ernest Hilgard and Josephine Hilgard*
The Brain that Changes Itself *Norman Doidge*
Your Body's Many Cries for Water *Dr. F Batmangheldj*

Clem Turner has worked as a clinical and cognitive behavioural hypnotherapist for many years. He is an

accredited member of the National Council for Hypnotherapy and a senior member of the General Hypnotherapy Register. He works from his therapy rooms in Sutton in Ashfield and at a clinic for complementary therapies in Mansfield, Nottinghamshire. Clem specialises in Pain Management; Stress and Anxiety Management and IBS. He is a certified provider of The Listening Programme (a programme to help children with learning difficulties) with Advanced Brain Technologies.

For a number of years now he has been running a series of CPD recognised workshops for qualified hypnotherapists with his wife Margaret Turner. The workshops include Pain Management, Anxiety Management, Weight Management, Smoking Cessation, Conversational Hypnosis/Influence, Mindfulness, Parts Therapy, Using HCBT and Advanced Skills for Newly Qualified Hypnotherapists. Clem is now also offering one to one sessions for Recording and Producing CD's. For more information please telephone 01623 556234 or e-mail Clem at: clem@clemturner.co.uk

Chapter Eight

Irritable Bowel Syndrome

Debbie Waller gives the background to understanding what Irritable Bowel Syndrome is and how hypnotherapy can help control this common and painful condition.

Although this is not intended to be a medical handbook, before working with IBS (Irritable Bowel Syndrome) you do need to understand something about the medical issues around it.

In medical terms, a syndrome is simply a technical term for a collection of symptoms. Obviously enough, Irritable Bowel Syndrome is characterised by a number of symptoms which occur around the bowel and digestive system, although these are not the same for every person diagnosed with the syndrome. It is also sometimes referred to as 'spastic colon'.

IBS is a condition or disorder, not a disease. This means it's not something you can catch or pass on, but a malfunction in the way your gut works. IBS is thought by most doctors to be associated with increased sensitivity in the lining of the gut but a single or specific cause has not yet been identified. The increased sensitivity has been connected with a number of factors, for example symptoms may develop after a bout of gastro-intestinal illness or food poisoning, or after a change in the nociceptive system, which controls how we feel pain.

At other times the symptoms may be triggered by a change in the body's ability to move food through the digestive system, or increased levels of stress. In fact, around half of IBS sufferers say their symptoms began after a stressful event.

Food allergies and intolerances, or a change in colonic flora (the 'friendly bacteria' living in the gut) have also been implicated in some cases.

IBS can develop at any age, including in childhood, but typically it starts between the ages of 20 and 30, and more women than men seek help from their GP. Around 20 per cent of the population is thought to be affected at some point in their lives, though as many people are said to self diagnose and self treat it's impossible to be exact, and the true figure may be higher.

The main symptoms

For most people, the main symptoms of Irritable Bowel Syndrome are abdominal pain along with either constipation or diarrhoea. Some people may experience both constipation and diarrhoea at different times, or the pain alone.

There are often other symptoms too, such as bloating, abdominal cramps, spasms, belching or flatulence, sudden and urgent needs for the toilet, mucous in the stools, dizziness, nausea, tiredness and headaches. The symptoms are not present constantly, but may come and go. They can disappear for months or even years, but as IBS is a lifelong condition there is always the possibility that they will recur. Different people find that different circumstances trigger off an episode of IBS - stress, anxiety, exercise, certain foods, caffeine or nicotine are common triggers - and symptoms may range from being quite mild to very severe.

Symptoms in men and women are broadly similar, though men tend to be less likely to report bloating, distension and feelings of incomplete evacuation (a sensation that they haven't 'finished' when emptying their bowels).

Many women find their IBS symptoms get worse when they are menstruating (having a period); this may be because of hormone changes, or because women may simply be more aware of changes in their abdominal region, especially at this time. Pregnancy often causes a reduction in IBS symptoms, as does the menopause, although neither birth control pills nor HRT appears to have any effect.

There seems to be less research on Irritable Bowel Syndrome in men, though there is some. One study showed that in younger men IBS seemed to be connected with higher than average levels of testosterone.

Emotional effects

Although IBS is a physical condition it is often associated with emotional issues as well. These are associated with its potential or actual influence on the sufferer's lifestyle. Stress and anxiety are foremost of these because of their connection with the operation of the gut.

We become stressed when the demands placed on us by life or the environment are more than we think we can cope with. This sets off a response in our body sometimes called the 'fight or flight' syndrome or the 'stress response'. Hormones and neurotransmitters (brain chemicals) put our body on high alert, ready to deal with an emergency.

Unfortunately we evolved this response at a time when emergencies generally meant a short term life threatening situation, like a predator jumping out on us or a rock fall, so we get ready to run away or fight back. Nowadays, stressful situations are generally longer term and mean we need to be calm, think and plan, exactly the opposite of what our bodies prepare us to do. This is why stress is such a problem.

70 per cent of people find stress and anxiety affect their digestive system - waiting for an interview you may need to visit the toilet more often, or notice 'butterflies' in your tummy. Those with IBS usually find that stress can cause a flare up of their symptoms; one study found that over a three month period, 52%

of patients who experienced a flare up of IBS symptoms reported high levels of stress, compared with only 29% of those who stayed symptom free.

Other studies have shown that those diagnosed with IBS may cope less well with stressful situations, increasing the likelihood of them reporting high levels of stress.

In addition, the symptoms of IBS may in themselves become a cause for stress or anxiety. Those who know they might need a toilet urgently or without notice can become unwilling to leave home or to socialise. This will be more intense if they have ever actually experienced public incontinence. Holidays, day trips, parties and meals out can be a nightmare for anyone whose symptoms are controlled by dietary restrictions. Painful cramps, fevers and diarrhoea can lead to regular time off work, which can lead to increased worrying about finances or job security.

Psychological symptoms

Anxiety UK say that say around 60 per cent of IBS patients who suffer psychological symptoms have Generalised Anxiety Disorder, another 20 per cent have depression, and the rest have other disorders. Like the physical symptoms, the seriousness of emotional issues ranges from mild to severe; Professor Whorwell, creator of the Manchester Model of Gut Directed Hypnotherapy says: "there is evidence that [IBS] patients have an extraordinarily high prevalence of suicidal ideation which is not necessarily related to depression." (Miller, Hopkins & Whorwell, 2004).

So although it's not always clear whether stress and anxiety are the cause or an effect of IBS, we can be confident that they frequently occur together.

The symptoms associated with IBS can also indicate other, potentially quite serious, medical issues. As hypnotherapists it's not ethical for us to diagnose medical conditions, so before working with anyone who tells you they have IBS make sure they have seen their GP to rule out these other possibilities. A medical diagnosis of IBS used to require a colonoscopy, which many people found to be a scary thought. Some people avoided going for to their doctor for this reason. However, IBS is now most often diagnosed through the 'Rome III' criteria, as recommended by NICE (National Institute for Clinical Excellence) which generally requires only symptom testing and blood tests.

IBS treatments

Once properly diagnosed, IBS treatments generally focus on reducing the symptoms. Regular anti-spasmodic medication can be prescribed by a medical practitioner to help prevent attacks, in addition suitable laxatives or anti-diarrhoeals can be used to control symptoms.

Many people find lifestyle changes can help reduce the number of attacks, these might include taking regular exercise, ensuring adequate sleep, quitting smoking, and dietary changes. As symptoms and triggers vary from one person to another, the GP is best placed to advise which of these might be most appropriate.

For example some people have already tried high fibre diets but these can be counter productive; avoiding cereal based fibre is often recommended. Stress management and relaxation techniques are also often advised and this is where the role of hypnotherapy starts to become clearer.

The functioning of those systems in the body which are automatic, like digestion, is controlled by the autonomic nervous system. This is divided into the sympathetic nervous system (which is involved with the 'fight or flight' response mentioned earlier) and the parasympathetic nervous system which is activated during relaxation.

Food moves through the digestive system by means of

alternating contractions and relaxations of the gut - a process called 'peristalsis'. If the sympathetic nervous system is over active, the gut can lose its natural rhythm and go into spasm. This spasm not only causes pain, it can block the transit of food or push it through too fast, causing the constipation or diarrhoea associated with IBS.

When the body enters a deeply relaxed state, the parasympathetic system takes over and the gut relaxes, allowing the food to move through normally and the painful symptoms to subside. Although this is somewhat simplified it does imply that relaxation might be helpful in reducing IBS and in fact a large number of studies have confirmed that deep relaxation, hypnotherapy, meditation and guided imagery can all help to alleviate the symptoms.

The NICE guidelines (paragraph 1.2.3.1) say:

"Referral for psychological interventions (cognitive behavioural therapy [CBT], hypnotherapy and/or psychological therapy) should be considered for people with IBS who do not respond to pharmacological treatments after 12 months and who develop a continuing symptom profile (described as refractory IBS)."

Despite this recommendation, in my experience most clients who come to hypnotherapists are self funded. These clients may come sooner than the 12 months indicated and as long as all other possible causes of their symptoms have been ruled out by a physician there is no ethical objection to working with them. The reason for the delay is said to be the relative expense of providing hypnotherapy compared with drug interventions, and the fact that there is only an evidence base for working with refractory IBS.

Models of hypnotherapy treatment

The best known protocol for using hypnotherapy with IBS, and the original evidence base referred to, is probably the Manchester Model, developed by Professor Peter Whorwell, Professor of Medicine and Gastroenterology at Manchester University. This model (also called Gut Directed Hypnotherapy or Gut Oriented Metaphor) uses visualisation and hypnosis to teach relaxation and pain control techniques, reduce stress and put patients in control of their IBS symptoms.

Professor Whorwell showed it was effective in reducing IBS symptoms and improving quality of life for 70-80% of his patients. It had the added benefit of continuing to work after the treatments stopped; the same was not the case with medication. It's not yet possible to predict which patients will respond the best, although it's suggested that hypnotisability does not appear to be a factor in how successful the treatment is.

Dr Whorwell's original study required people to undertake up to twelve sessions over a three month period. They used deep relaxation techniques and repetition of a scripted metaphor centred on a river which represented the gut.

Clients were asked to clear out rubbish to allow it to run freely if they suffered from IBS with constipation, or to shore it up and allow it to run more slowly and smoothly if they suffered diarrhoea. A version of glove anaesthesia familiar to many hypnotherapists was used to relieve pain. The programme also included giving people a good explanation of how their gut works, and encouraging them to use a CD at home. Since the publication of this study, other studies have been published supporting its findings.

In addition, alternative protocols have been developed, many by hypnotherapists rather than gastro-enterologists. These have not undergone the same kind of testing as the original Manchester Model study but are broadly based on the findings of the studies.

For example, OPSIM (On-going Progressive Session Induction

Method) was developed by Michael Mahoney, a clinical hypnotherapist and winner of several Innovation & Research Awards for his work in IBS. OPSIM was developed to avoid the repetition of identical sessions involved in the original Manchester Study as Mahoney suggests 'simple repetition of the same single session often ingrained, rather than released the presenting negative thoughts and feelings'. Up to six interlinked sessions are undertaken, each one different and building on the one before.

Whereas the Manchester Model focussed solely on the physical symptoms of IBS, OPSIM includes work on reducing anxiety and other peripheral emotional issues as well.

Another option is the Life Solutions Six Session approach developed by the Academy of Clinical and Medical Hypnosis. This also has elements designed to deal with the stress and emotional impact of living with IBS, specifically it integrates cognitive behavioural techniques within the hypnotherapy.

Duncan Murray of Solent Hypnotherapy, an IBS sufferer himself, has developed a treatment programme which he suggests works best with four weeks therapy followed by self-maintenance at home. He says that in his approach 'the separate processes of the 'Manchester Model' have been transformed from a medical hypnotic approach to a more naturalistic one of story-telling' (http://the-ibs-treatment.com/FAQs.html) and there is a much greater emphasis on metaphor.

If you wish to work with IBS you may choose to learn one or more of these protocols as part of your continuous professional development.

However, it's perfectly possible to put together an effective programme for working with IBS based on the principles offered by the research and your knowledge of how hypnotherapy works. The suggestions for approaching this issue here are just such an option.

Ethical and safety conditions

There are, as always, ethical and safety considerations when working with a medical condition.
- When you talk to clients or advertise, avoid using words like 'treat' or 'cure' which imply you can take away the underlying medical problem. Make it clear to potential clients that IBS is a life long condition but that hypnotherapy might be able to help them control or reduce the symptoms.
- Don't make any claims for hypnotherapy that you can't substantiate, refer clients to the published studies if they ask for evidence. Make it clear whether you use the exact approach mentioned in the studies or not.
- Check that the client's IBS has been diagnosed by a medical professional and not by the client themselves, because the symptoms can also indicate other conditions which need to be ruled out before hypnotherapy goes ahead.
- Clients should be asked to check that their GP has no objections to them using hypnotherapy. Your professional body may require you to get a written referral, check with them before you begin to work with IBS clients.
- Clients should be referred back to their GP if they develop new symptoms or their existing symptoms worsen.

Red flag symptoms

A medical referral applies in particular to symptoms which the British Society of Gastroenterology identifies as 'red flag' indicators that need urgent further investigation:
- A change in bowel habit - especially in people over the age 40
- Passing blood from the back passage
- Unintentional weight loss of more than 2 kg (4 pounds)
- Diarrhoea which interrupts sleep
- Fever

- NICE also includes a family history of bowel or ovarian cancer as a red flag indicator

Although the NICE guidelines say hypnotherapy should only be considered for those whose IBS has not responded to drug treatments after 12 months, clients may well approach you before this length of time has passed. There is no problem with working with them if the other ethical and safety conditions are met.

In the vast majority of cases all these issues can be clarified on the phone or by email when the client makes the initial contact, and they will not pose a problem.

Having ensured that it is safe and ethical for you to work with your client, begin by listening to them in detail. As you do with all clients, pick up on their modalities, the metaphors they give you when describing their condition and symptoms, how their IBS affects their lives on an everyday basis. It's handy to have a questionnaire for this in addition to your usual intake form. It can be sent to clients before the first session, or filled in with them when you meet, and gives you plenty of personal and relevant information to include in your healing suggestions.

Developing your own protocol

The advantage of developing your own protocol is that you can be responsive to the individual needs of your client, although a course of hypnotherapy is likely to include:
- Deep relaxation
- The use of healing metaphors
- Hypnotic pain control
- Anxiety reduction and stress management techniques
- Consolidation and future pacing

As already mentioned, the Manchester Model of Gut Oriented Metaphor required patients to undergo up to 12 sessions of hypnotherapy, but in my experience few private clients will want or need this many. A good quality of life improvement can often be made in four to six sessions.

Typical course of treatment
A typical course of therapy might be arranged as follows:

Session one: intake.
This will be arranged in much the same way as a first session with any client, focussed on gathering information, answering the client's questions, correcting any misconceptions about hypnosis and building rapport. I begin therapy with relaxation, so a progressive muscular relaxation induction, deepener plus teaching deep breathing, self hypnosis, meditation or other relaxation techniques. The client is asked to practice at home before the next session.

Session two: healing metaphors
You will find a number of different metaphors which can be used, or you may be able to write your own, perhaps based on your client's interests or experiences.

Duncan Murray (http://the-ibs-treatment.com) suggests a warm, sunny walled garden which of course represents the body. There is a stream running through the garden which represents the gut. If the client has IBS with constipation, the stream is blocked by debris and fallen branches from the garden so the water is damming up and unable to flow.

If the client has IBS with diarrhoea then the stream is silted up, narrowed with broken sides so the water is running too fast, like rapids. In either case the client, having explored the garden, is asked to remove their shoes and socks and move up and down the stream righting the problems it so it runs naturally and easily again. The garden contains a large tree, to represent protective strength and health, under which the client can rest and restore themselves after these exertions.

Session three: pain control
Any hypnotherapy pain control method can be appropriate.

I most often use glove anaesthesia which involves using suggestion to numb one of the client's hands, then transferring the numbness to the painful area. Glove anaesthesia when used in dental hypnosis often uses a sensation of cold to numb the hand but when working with IBS warmth seems to be better. Many IBS sufferers report using a hot water bottle on their stomach brings relief from the pain, and using suggestions of warmth in the hypnotic session ties in with this expectation.

Session four: stress and anxiety
At this point, most clients are already experiencing improvements in the severity and/or duration of their IBS symptoms.

They should be regularly listening to your CDs or practising other relaxation methods at home. The side effect of this is that their stress and anxiety may have lessened already, but it's nonetheless valuable to have at least one session specifically on this topic.

Revisit your intake form and look at where the majority of their stress comes from, dealing with this as you would with any client who is suffering the negative effects of stress. As NICE recommend CBT (cognitive behavioural therapy) for IBS as well as hypnotherapy I prioritise cognitive type techniques: stress diaries, identifying and challenging negative thought patterns and core beliefs, teaching and rehearsing new coping behaviours, positive reinforcement of improvements, and so on.

Further sessions: what does your client need?
Depending on the client's circumstances, you may need more than one session to successfully reduce their stress and anxiety.

Some clients need additional support such as increasing motivation to adopt the lifestyle modifications advised by their doctor.

This might include quitting smoking and making changes to their diet and exercise regimes (whether or not they need to reduce their weight). Especially if the client's lifestyle has been restricted by IBS for any length of time, they may also benefit from some work on improving confidence or self esteem. Protocols for helping with these issues will be dealt with elsewhere in this book and there is no need to repeat them here.

If you do not get the improvements you expected, it is worth considering whether some deeper issue, such as resistance or secondary gain, is at work. By saying this, I'm definitely not implying that the client is deliberately blocking success, exaggerating their symptoms or 'faking' their condition. However, for some, the unconscious mind perceives benefits in the continuation of their IBS; either it gets them something they want (such as sympathy or attention) or it allows them to avoid something they don't want (such as work or social occasions).

In this case, you could consider a more analytical approach using parts, regression or similar techniques to uncover and release the underlying issue. It's only fair to say that in suggesting this I am stepping away from the published evidence supporting the use of hypnotherapy for IBS; studies have focussed only on relaxation, metaphor and cognitive behavioural techniques. However, these are classic hypnotherapy tools, and if your client is aware of this and willing to continue therapy, the change of direction may help them benefit from your symptom reduction programme.

Holding sessions weekly or fortnightly gives your client time to compete the homework and see improvements, whilst keeping the momentum going. I also recommend asking them to commit to a block of sessions at the beginning rather than one at a time. Although they may get some symptom relief fairly quickly, in order to get the best long term result they need to persevere. This can be encouraged by judicious use of a discount for those who pay in advance for a number of sessions.

And finally, although I've suggested what seems to me a logical progression through the therapy, you can of course, deal with the various issues in whichever order seems most useful to your client. I give homework at every session - listening to CDs or practising the techniques we've covered in the session is a must, and keeping an IBS diary can be useful.

I also strongly recommend the regular use of SUDS (subjective units of distress scale) in the diary and at every session. For those not familiar with this scale it means asking your client to rate their symptoms on a scale of one to ten. Being able to measure improvements gives a confidence boost to both you and your client.

REFERENCES:

Academy of Clinical and Medical Hypnosis
http://ukhypnotherapy.org/
Anxiety UK http://www.anxietyuk.org.uk
British Society of Gastroenterology http://www.bsg.org.uk
Duncan Murray, Solent Hypnotherapy http://www.solent-hypnotherapy.co.uk/Irritable%20Bowel%20Syndrome.pdf
IBS Care http://ibs-care.org/pdfs/ref_143.pdf
Michael Mahoney Hypnotherapy
www.michaelmahoneyhypnotherapist.com
National Institute for Clinical Excellence (NICE) 2008 guidelines CG61: Irritable bowel syndrome in adults: Diagnosis and management of irritable bowel syndrome in primary care.
http://publications.nice.org.uk/irritable-bowel-syndrome-in-adults-cg61/introduction

Walled Garden Script:

This script is based on an idea by Duncan Murray DCHyp of ibshelp.org.uk
[This version is for a client with diarrhoea, if your client has constipation, change the stream so it is filled with rocks and debris, backing up as if it were dammed.
Use the induction of your choice, usually one based in relaxation.]

Imagine yourself standing out in the open air on a beautiful summer day. In front of you, you see an old set of five stone steps ... at the bottom of the steps you can just see a wall, and in the wall is a door.

You begin to feel curious, eager to explore, and you approach the top of the steps. Your footing feels safe and secure, there's a handrail there if you choose to run your hand along it, and as you step down onto the first step you notice a feeling of peace and tranquillity.

Imagine those steps in whatever way you wish, perhaps you notice the sound of your footstep on the stone as you step down again onto the second step, or perhaps the feel of the handrail under the palm of your hand. As you descend you breathe clean fresh air, the sun warms and calms you, and you relax more with every step.

Go down now onto the third step, noticing that wonderful feeling of peace and calm getting stronger as you descend - stronger and stronger, relaxing more and more.

Continue descending, down onto the fourth step now, deeper and deeper into that relaxation, feeling safe, secure and comfortable.

And as you drift down onto the fifth and last step you find yourself descending into a more profound sense of relaxation and comfort than you have felt in a long time ... maybe even allowing yourself to be more relaxed than you have ever been ... relaxing more and more deeply.

You're standing now in front of the door in the wall that you noticed from the top of the steps. Pay attention to that door, notice its colour and shape, the door handle and how it is set into the wall. Reach out your hand, rest it on the door handle, noticing whether it may be warmed by the sun, or cool in the shadow here at the bottom of the steps.

Use the handle and open the door, feeling its weight as you easily push it wide open and step through into a beautiful garden completely enclosed by the wall you have just passed through. Close the door behind you, hearing the click as it shuts, and begin to notice the garden around you.

It's summer here too and if anything it seems even warmer here than outside the walls. You are surrounded by beautiful flowers. All your favourite ones are growing here. Notice their shapes and colours, the different greens of the leaves, the wonderful scents of the blooms carried to you on a warm, gentle breeze.

You can reach out and touch those flowers if you wish, enjoying the sensation of their softness against the tips of your fingers, or bend for a moment to enjoy that perfume even more clearly.

Perhaps not too far away you can hear the rustling of leaves on the bushes growing here, as they are touched by the breeze, or perhaps you become aware of the pleasant song of birds as they rest in the garden.

Above you the summer sky is a clear blue, with a few soft, white fluffy clouds floating past ... notice them for a moment, maybe they remind you of childhood games, seeing images and shapes in the clouds as they drift lazily by.

You can begin to explore this garden now, moving anywhere you wish to go. Notice the ground beneath your feet as you move *around. Perhaps you hear the crunch of gravel underfoot, your footsteps ringing clear on paving, or silent on grass. This is your garden and it can be anything you like.*

Notice the way the garden is laid out, - formal, structured and ordered, or perhaps simply left to nature, the plants growing riotously wherever they choose.

In the centre of the garden you find a tree, large and old but strong and healthy, its branches soaring up into the blue sky. Stand under the tree for a moment, taking into yourself some of its calm peaceful nature, feeling sheltered and protected.

Not far away you hear water, a little stream passes through the garden, placed there to allow the water to soak into the rich soil keeping the flowers hydrated and healthy, just as the food you eat passes through your gut, passing the nutrients into the muscles, nerves, fibres and cells of your body.

From where you stand you can hear that the stream is turbulent, fast, and although the sound of water is pleasant it seems to run too fast, rushing the water away before the plants can absorb the moisture they require.

You walk around the tree and find the stream, as you expected it's tumbling along in its narrow stream bed, and the turbulence is tearing at the sides of the stream bed, stirring up mud and debris, clouding and polluting the stream. You realise that just as the flow in your gut needs to be regulated to keep your body strong and healthy, the health and well being of your beautiful garden depend on regulating the flow of water in this stream.

You remove your shoes and socks, feeing the warmth of the sun on your feet as you do so, and safely and securely enter the stream. The water comes just to the tops of your feet .. it swirls around your feet but you stand in it securely and steadily. The water is warmed slightly by the sun and feels pleasant, refreshing, on your feet and toes.

Explore the stream, moving downstream at first, as far as the garden walls. You find that in places the stream is almost blocked, branches, rocks and other obstructions narrow the channel. You realise that where the water is allowed to flow freely it moves more slowly, gently, but as it passes through these blocked and narrowed places the volume of water is forced into a narrower path to the point that the water rushes through like rapids.

You begin to remove these obstacles, one by one, feeling with your hands and feet to discover them all, even those which are under the surface and cannot be seen. You lift even the largest easily, throwing them far away from the stream so they cannot possibly fall back in. As you do so, the water begins to move more calmly, able to spread to the full width of the stream bed - no longer under pressure it moves more slowly, the rushing slows to a gentle movement which is calming and relaxing. As the movement of the water slows, it clears, you begin to notice how clean and sparkling it is becoming.

When you reach the garden wall, turn around and see the stream from a new perspective. The part you have cleared is running steadily and smoothly, upstream of where you first entered is still roiling and rushing so you make you way back to that point and begin to clear the area upstream too as far as you can. Move up and down the stream, removing everything that blocks its smooth, steady passage, noticing and disposing of those last few items you may have missed on the first time through.

When you have finished clearing the stream, you can step out of the water, noting with a sense of satisfaction the slow gentle pace of it now, the slow, soothing movements and the soft musical sounds. You look along the length of the stream from one side of the garden to the other and notice a feeling of pride as you see it flowing more quietly and smoothly, and as the water becomes clearer you can become aware of the fact that the health of the stream reflects the health of your gut and that the clearer, quieter and smoother the flow of the water in the stream, the healthier and happier your gut is.

You notice from here on the bank that some of the plants grow very close to the edge, so close that from time to time they may drop more leaves, twigs or obstacles into the stream and perhaps even threaten to make it run faster again. However, you also know that now you're aware of the problem you can check the stream from time to time, and keep it clear, the flow remaining smooth and gentle and calm.

Go back to the main part of the garden, and sit under the beautiful tree you noticed before. Just allow yourself to relax comfortably, sinking even deeper into a wonderful sense of relaxation and wellbeing. Stretch out your legs and as you do so notice that your lower body and abdomen are warmed by the sunshine even while your face is kept cool by the shade of the tree. Notice the warmth of the sunshine on your tummy in particular, how warm and soothing it is.

Imagine that warmth passing through your clothing, the layers of skin and into the organs beneath giving a sense of comfort and ease. Letting yourself drift deeper and deeper in to that sense of relaxation, you become aware of the tree above you, how it has both flexibility and strength and how these things help it to grow. The tree can move with the natural forces around it or stand firm to withstand them, changing and adapting its approach, and you feel more and more confident that you can do the same, dealing creatively and effectively with the pressures and changes in your life.

Be aware that just as the leaf canopy stretches above you the roots delve and spread down into the earth, a kind of symmetry, the roots underground as large and complex as the branches above with yourself on the mirror point, between the two. The roots absorb the water, minerals and nutrients from the stream you cleared, so much more easily now it runs more slowly and gently.

The warmth of the sun on your tummy continues to soothe and relax you and you can spend some time there just soaking up the wonderful, peaceful atmosphere, feeling more calm and in control than you have felt in a long time, letting the warmth soak into your body and relieve any pain or discomfort you felt, increasing your sense of ease and comfort, drawing on the strength of the tree above you.

[pause]

And now I want you to imagine opening your eyes in that garden, taking a long look around it, knowing that although it's time for you to come back to the present time and place you can always return here any time you choose, each time you come you will find it easier to clear that stream, and find that it remains clear for longer.

For now, though you notice your feet are dry, the sun has dried them while you relaxed so you can replace your shoes and socks, and return to the garden door. Take a last look around, and go out through the door, locking it behind you. Place the key in a safe place so no one else can come here, and find the steps you came down.

You are going to climb those steps, as I count to five, one step each time I count, and although you will bring that sense of peace and contentment you found in the garden with you, you will be more aware of the her and now wider awake with each number and each step.

Until, when I get to five and ask you to open your eyes you'll be wide awake, refreshed, relaxed, feeling really good.

Awakening:
One, coming back with your head clear
Two, coming back with your mind refreshed and relaxed
Three, coming back with your body warm and comfortable
Four, at the next number I'll ask you to open your eyes. When you

do you'll be fully awake, fully aware, feeling better than you have in a long time
Five, eyes open, wide awake.

Since qualifying as a hypnotherapist and stress management coach, Debbie Waller has run a busy hypnotherapy and stress management practice in Yorkshire, UK. Although she sees people with other issues, she has a particular interest in working with stress and the related areas such as phobias, anxiety and Irritable Bowel Syndrome. She works mostly with one to one clients but also regularly provides seminars and stress management training to local businesses and groups.

Debbie taught for a nationwide therapy training organisation for three years alongside her therapy practice before launching her own school, Yorkshire Hypnotherapy Training. She currently divides her time between working with clients, training therapists and running an online magazine for student and practising hypnotherapists. Contact Debbie at www.hypnotherapy-for-ibs.co.uk

the hypnotherapy handbook

the hypnotherapy handbook

Index

Advertising 47
Advertising budget 48
Acute pain 158
Addiction, chemicals 101
Anxiety, definition of 62
Anxiety number of sessions 85
Anxiety, symptoms of 68
Agoraphobia 140

Belief systems 76
Binge eating 133
Branding, stationery 41
Branding, you 42
Boundaries 25
Burnout 29
Business websites 38

Calibrating feelings 72
Client perceptions, you as expert 100
CPD 33

Diet, lifestyle and pain 165
Dopamine, artificial production of, 102

Ecology check 24
Emotional pain 158

Index

Empowering clients 113
Excuses 129
Exercise, importance of 127
Eye movement integration 70, 78
Family 24
Fight and flight response 63
Future pacing 146
Full time career 23

GAD 7 74
General Anxiety Disorder (GAD) 67
Getting known 41

Hypnotherapist, maintaining ideal weight 122

IBS, emotional effects 175
IBS, symptoms of 174
IBS, typical course of treatment 183
Image 28
Impact of marketing 48
Irritable bowel syndrome 173

Lack of motivation 133
Life solutions, approach to IBS 180
Local 49

Index

Negative outcomes, working with 82
NICE guidelines 178
Nicheing 30

Manchester model 176
Marketing, time needed 37
Motivational hypnotherapy 126
Motivational tools 135

Obsessive-compulsive disorder (OCD) 67

Panic Disorder 67
Pain 157
Pain, characteristics of 158
Pain, statistics 158
Pain relief 160
Pain, planning sessions 169
Phobias 139
Phobia, NLP 142
Phobias, number of sessions 144
Phobias, therapy structure 147
Photographs 42
PHQ-9 74
Potential clients 38
Post traumatic stress disorder 67
Preparing sessions, importance of 109

Index

Press releases 52
Professional self 24
Professional organisations 34
Protocol 182
Print advertising 39

Questioning techniques 74

Rapport 71, 164
Referred pain 158
Reflective diary 32
Regression 185
Removing pain, when 163

Secondary gain 170, 185
Self hypnosis 113, 130
Self sabotage 170
Simple phobia 140
Smoking cessation 98
Smoking, role of memory 104
Smoking, structure of treatment 105
Social anxiety disorder 67
Social media 58
Social phobia 140
Solution focus 147
Specific phobias 66

Index

Straight talking 128
Stress definition of, 65
Stress hormones 64
Submodalities 75
SUDS scales 186
Supervision importance of 30

Tasking between sessions 89
Time Line reframing 150
Time management 26
Thought stopping 112
Triggers for smoking 103

Unconscious, role of 64
USP 38

Virtual gastric band 123

Websites 53
Weight loss, ABC 123
Weight loss, the 80-20 plan 134
When is therapy finished? 88
'Wordweaving' 95

Useful websites

Professional resources

National Council for Hypnotherapy

http://www.hypnotherapists.org.uk

General Hypnotherapy Register

http://www.general-hypnotherapy-register.com

The Hypnotherapy Directory

http://www.hypnotherapy-directory.org.uk

The Complementary and Natural Healthcare Council

http://www.cnhc.org.uk

National Guild of Hypnotists

https://ngh.net

Hypnothoughts

http://www.hypnothoughts.com

Useful websites

Author's websites

Ann Jaloba
http://www.wellthought.co.uk
http://www.supervisionplus.org

Cathy Simmons
http://www.cathysimmons.co.uk

Clem Turner
http://www.clemturner.co.uk

Debbie Waller
http://www.debbiewaller.com
http://www.hypnotherapy-for-ibs.co.uk

Deborah Pearce
http://www.deborahpearce.co.uk
http://www.therapistsmarketingsolutions.co.uk

Fiona Nicolson
http://www.fionanicolson.com

Nicola Griffiths
http://www.nicolagriffiths.co.uk
http://www.therapistsmarketingsolutions.co.uk

Useful websites

Pat Duckworth
http://www.roystonhypnotherapy.co.uk
http://www.patduckworth.com/cognitive-hypnotherapy

Steve Miller
http://www.stevemillerhypnotherapy.co.uk
http://hypnotherapybusinessschool.co.uk

Helping you to help your clients

Visit

The Hypnotherapy Handbook website

http://hypnotherapyhandbook.com/

All the information on forthcoming events linked with the book

the hypnotherapy handbook

Printed in Great Britain
by Amazon